What others are saying about this book:

"Management of Aggressive Behavior *which addresses a much needed and often overlooked concern with regard to the use of force is a rare commodity in police training.*"
— Mildred "Missy" O'Linn
Police Defense Attorney
Franscell, Strickland, Roberts
and Lawrence
Pasadena, California

"Management of Aggressive Behavior *provides the experience base to successfully recognize and control altercations before they begin, thus allowing all parties to come away winners!*"
— Officer Dennis F. Jurasz
North Tonawanda (NY) Pol. Dept.

"Management of Aggressive Behavior *is an excellent tool for human services professionals to use in achieving successful interactions, minimizing injuries, and instilling a higher degree of confidence. I highly recommend this book to anyone dealing with violent people in their work and in their lives.*"
— Bonnie S. Michelman
Vice President
International Association for
Healthcare Security and Safety
Bosto

D1247748

"Management of Ag͏͏͏ ͏͏͏ ͏͏͏s as a *foundation for all oth͏͏͏ ͏͏͏ ͏͏͏raining by providing the offic͏͏͏ ͏͏͏ ͏͏͏ "early warning system" when dealing with the potentially volatile situations that they encounter every day.*"
— Harry C. Kinne III
Director of Public Safety
Wesleyan University
Middletown, Connecticut

Management of Aggressive Behavior

A comprehensive guide to learning how to recognize, reduce, manage, and control aggressive behavior.

by

Roland Ouellette

PERFORMANCE DIMENSIONS PUBLISHING
P.O. Box 502, Powers Lake, WI 53159-0502

Management of Aggressive Behavior

A comprehensive guide to learning how
to recognize, reduce, manage, and
control aggressive behavior.

by

Roland Ouellette

Published by:

PERFORMANCE DIMENSIONS PUBLISHING
a division of Performance Dimensions, Inc.

P.O. Box 502, Powers Lake, WI 53159-0502, U.S.A.
Phone (414) 279-3850

Copyright © 1993 by Performance Dimensions, Inc.
First Printing: April, 1993
Printed in the United States of America

Library of Congress Cataloging-in-Publication Data

Ouellette, Roland, 1937-
     Management of aggressive behavior : acomprehensive guide to
learning how to recognize, reduce, manage, and control aggressive
behavior / by Roland Ouellette.
          p.   cm.
     Includes bibliographical references (p.   ) and index.
     ISBN 1-879411-22-9 : $14.95
     1. Aggressiveness (Psychology)--Prevention. 2. Violence-
-Prevention. 3. Human services--Psychological aspects.   I. Title.
BF575.A3088   1993   92-44600
155.2'32--dc20   CIP

Library of Congress Catalog Card Number: 92-85340
ISBN: 1-879411-18-0 $14.95 Softcover

Dedication

This book is dedicated: To all the professionals who have to deal with the continually rising number of assaultive and violent individuals.

To Debrah Garro for all her help.

And finally, to my children, Beth, Ellen, and Eric, for their encouragement.

Epigraph

"For to win one hundred victories in one hundred battles is not the acme of skill. To subdue the enemy without fighting is the acme of skill."

— Sun Tzu
500 BC

Contents

Foreword

I first had the opportunity to meet Roland Ouellette, the author of this book, in the early 1980's. I was initially impressed by his easy going demeanor and friendly smile. Almost instantly upon meeting him, he became my friend.

I learned that he is a master in knowing how to recognize and manage human aggression. He has developed a training program aptly named, "Management Of Aggressive Behavior." In this program he coupled his life experiences of successfully dealing with aggressive and hostile individuals with extensive research into the psychological and physiological aspects of human aggression.

In formulating the MOAB Training Program, Roland decided to focus on the "how to" rather than the "why." I have no doubt that I would rather know "how to" recognize an imminent assault than to know "why" an assault is imminent.

The MOAB Training Program has been hailed by virtually all those who have completed it as extremely beneficial. These comments have been received from police officers, teachers, emergency medical services personnel, firefighters, supervisors, security officers, corrections personnel, customer relations representatives, and a multitude of others that have to deal with the public under less than desirable circumstances.

Roland Ouellette, has "paid his dues." He has survived a career in law enforcement and corrections. This book could just as easily have been titled, "How Not To Fight." As a martial arts black belt in two separate disciplines, Roland knows that there are times when you must get physical.

Therefore, demonstrated in this book are various simple and effective techniques to physically control certain types of physical aggression.

If you understand human aggression and have the ability to recognize certain signals, you may be able to avoid many potentially physical altercations. You don't have to be a black belt like Roland to acquire the knowledge, confidence, and skill to manage aggressive behavior. You have these resources in the pages that follow.

Every once in a while there comes along a book that can have a very significant impact on society. I have no doubt that *Management of Aggressive Behavior*, or more simply, *MOAB*, is such a book and it will benefit virtually every man, woman, and child that reads it.

This book is much more than just another philosophical approach to understanding aggressive individuals written by an academic researcher with little or no practical experience. As you read the pages of *MOAB*, you will find that it is filled with practical knowledge, wisdom, insight, and physical skills. This is more than a book — it is a comprehensive blueprint of ways to recognize and manage human aggression.

Will what you learn in this book apply to all people under all circumstances? No! Human behavior and aggression are too varied and complex to be contained in one book. In addition, intelligence, cultural differences, and individual personality disorders negate some of the behavioral signs that indicate when aggression is imminent. However, what you read here, coupled with the book's many photos, will enable you to increase your knowledge, understanding, and skill in managing aggressive behavior whether you are young or old, big or small, man or woman.

Don't just read *MOAB*, absorb it for maximum benefits. This is not a "read once and pass on" type

of book. Read *MOAB* from cover to cover more
than once. Study it and refer to various sections
from time to time. You need to make the information and skill that you acquire from *MOAB* a part of
your life — an important part!

   The information that you learn from *MOAB*
will help you in more areas of your life than you may
realize. Wives will be able to deal with their husbands more effectively and husbands with their
wives. Parents, children, siblings, supervisors,
subordinates, and others can all make their lives
better by understanding the information contained
in *MOAB*.

   After reading *MOAB*, I'm sure you will agree
that Roland Ouellette has made a significant contri-
bution to our society's body of knowledge.

                            — Ed Nowicki, B.S., M.A.
                              Twin Lakes, Wisconsin

About Ed Nowicki: He is a nationally recognized
law enforcement training expert and author. He is
also the former executive director of the nation's
largest law enforcement training association, the
American Society of Law Enforcement Trainers
(ASLET).

Acknowledgement

The author would like to thank the many people who have assisted in the research of *Management of Aggressive Behavior* during the last thirty years. There are too many law enforcement, corrections, military, security, and health care personnel to list individually. However, listed below are just a few who have contributed their knowledge and skills:

My daughter and Vice President of R.E.B. Security Training, Inc., Ellen C. Ouellette, for the many hours of dedication to this book.

Attorney Mildred (Missy) O'Linn for her review on the proper use of force.

Attorney Thomas Collins for his editing efforts.

The members of the American Society of Law Enforcement Trainers (ASLET). This book would not have been possible without them.

My Karate instructors, Masutarsu Oyama and Gogen Yamagushi, who taught me to treat people with dignity.

The members of the Hartford Karate Club who have put up with my experimentations for the past thirty years: John Celentano; Tom Collins; Fred DiBattista; Wilson Keithline; Lou Pavan; Bill Puro; Ken Sheptoff; Dave Whitehead, M.D.; Dave Whitehead, Jr., D.M.D.; and Bill Whitehead.

The numerous members of the Northeast Colleges and University Association, Inc. (NECUSA); the American Society of Industrial Security (ASIS); the International Association for Healthcare Security and Safety (IAHSS); and the Monadnock PR-24® Training Council, Inc.

Introduction

The frequency of assaults on human services personnel continues to rise at an alarming rate each year. This increase in assaults is directly related to the escalation of incidents of alcohol and drug abuse, juvenile delinquency, gangs, and crime. The majority of assaults are with personal weapons, such as hands, fists, feet, or etc.

Management of Aggressive Behavior was written for human services personnel in response to this growing violence. All those involved in health care, security, law enforcement, public safety, corrections, environmental protection, and the military will benefit from the topics covered.

This is a book of options on how to recognize, reduce, manage, and control aggressive behavior. Understanding body language and recognizing the signals can prepare you for an attack before it occurs, end the confrontation before it begins, and help you win the encounter without physical confrontation.

Non-verbal and verbal communications skills are the foundation of all use of force options. This book was designed to give you additional alternatives to the knowledge and skills you may have already acquired.

This book was not designed to replace hands-on training programs, but to add insight into areas of growing importance. For further information about training programs, including MOAB and OCAT® (Oleoresin Capsicum Aerosol Training), contact R.E.B. Security Training, Inc., P.O. Box 697, Avon, CT 06001, or call (203) 677-5936 for assistance.

Warning—Disclaimer

The information, photos and graphics displayed in this book are intended to assist all those who are confronted with an aggressive individual. It is not the intention of the author, publisher, or any of their agents to encourage persecution of any single person, group, organization, or religion who are free to express themselves under the protection of the First Amendment of the Constitution of the United States.

This book is designed to provide information in regard to the subject matter covered. It is sold with the understanding that the authors and publisher are not engaged in rendering legal or other professional services. If legal or other professional assistance is required, the services of a competent professional should be sought.

It is not the purpose of this book to reprint all the information that is otherwise available to the authors and publisher, but to complement, amplify, and supplement other texts. You are urged to read all available material and to learn as much as possible about aggressive individuals and to tailor the information to your individual needs. For more information, see the "Bibliography" at the end of this book.

Every effort has been made to make this book as complete and as accurate as possible. However, there may be mistakes, both typographical and in content. Therefore, this text should be used only as a general guide and not as the ultimate source on the management of aggressive behavior. Furthermore, this book contains information only up to the printing date.

The purpose of this book is to educate, inform, and stimulate thought. The author and Performance Dimensions shall have neither liability nor responsibility to any person or entity with respect to any loss or damage caused, or alleged to be caused, directly or indirectly by the information contained in this book.

If you do not wish to be bound by the above, you may return this book to the publisher for a full refund.

Non-Verbal and Verbal Communications Skills

Introduction

Non-verbal and verbal signals are the most widely used forms of communication. Yet, these are the most often neglected areas of training. Human services personnel are frequently placed in danger of assault because they are unaware of the "non-verbal and verbal" signals given by aggressors. Research has shown that non-verbal and verbal skills are necessary to prevent most encounters where force is used. "Some experts think physical presence and communications skills alone could handle up to 98% of the incidents potentially requiring force."[1]

Body language, also referred to as kinesics, is defined as unconscious signals sent from the brain that outwardly reflects a person's emotional state. Significant research has been done in understanding body language; starting with Charles Darwin in the middle of the last century, to the Father of Kinesics, Ray Birdwhistell, in the 1950's, to Desmond Morris in the 1960's, and Allan Pease in the 1970's and 80's. Body language is a powerful communications tool that is complex and dynamic. The benefits of learning the secrets of body language are enormous.

People are constantly communicating on a subconscious level. Ray Birdwhistell, who carried out extensive body language studies in the 1950's, says, "Ten percent (10%) of the message we deliver to people is verbal, ninety percent (90%) is non-verbal."

If we learn to interpret correctly what we see, we can arm ourselves with a powerful tool that can increase our chances for a successful outcome. If we incorrectly interpret the information, it can trigger aggression with unexpected and disastrous consequences.

It is easier for people to lie with words than with their body language. Body language is much harder to control than words.

When verbal and non-verbal communications conflict, we should rely on the non-verbal signals. In order of importance, non-verbal signals can be divided into three key areas:

1.) Space
2.) Eye Contact
3.) Gestures and Posture

Each of these signals will be addressed in this book.

1

Space

Proxemics is defined as a branch of study dealing with the personal and cultural spatial needs of people and the interaction with that space within their environment. Throughout this book proxemics is referred to as space.

Space is made up of four oval-shaped zones that surround each of us and consists of the **intimate, personal, social,** and **public zones** (see Chart 1 in the Chart section).

Personal Space

Personal space can be described as an area surrounding us which others are generally not expected to intrude upon and consists of the intimate and personal zones. These two zones cause us the

most problems when dealing with aggressive individuals. The importance of personal space cannot
be stressed enough. Without recognizing the importance of the intimate and personal zones, we
run the risk of increasing other people's anxiety
and significantly decreasing our own ability to react
properly to an assault.

As shown in the Chart 1, the intimate zone is
approximately 18 inches in front of us and the
personal zone is approximately 3 feet in front of us.
The distance of these zones to the side of us is
approximately 1 1/2 feet and 5 feet to the rear of
us. Following are some examples of how the
intimate and personal zones are affected when a
person enters our space from the front, side, or
rear.

■ **Example of personal space to the front:** If
someone other than a friend or family
member approaches us from the front, even
in a friendly manner, and comes closer than
3 feet, we normally feel uncomfortable. This
is because that person has "violated our
space." Our reaction may be to move away,
tighten our facial muscles, or open and
close our fists.

■ **Example of personal space to the side:**
Generally, we will not face strangers in an
elevator because it makes us feel uncomfortable. Instead, we stand side by side.
The explanation for this is simple: our personal space to the side is much smaller
than it is to the front, so others can come
closer to us without making us feel uncomfortable.

■ **Example of personal space to the rear:** Our
personal space to the rear is the largest.

We require more space behind us when being approached by a stranger than from either the front or side. If we are approached from the rear by someone who is walking in the same direction, even when that person is a good distance away, it makes us feel uncomfortable. This is because we require the most space to the rear.

A good example of this is when choosing a seat in a restaurant. If given a choice, most people will choose to sit with their backs to the wall instead of their backs to the other tables. There is no need to protect the large oval space behind us because the wall is protecting us.

Personal space varies with each person based on differences in culture, environment, personal habits, gender, and age. The following is a brief description of each:

■ **Cultural differences:** People who were raised in crowded cities or environments usually have smaller personal zones, while those raised in the country have larger personal zones. City people may feel comfortable when someone enters their personal space, but people from the country may become extremely anxious.

■ **Environmental differences:** We protect our personal environments, such as our bedrooms, offices, cars, hospital rooms, dorm rooms, or cells as much as we protect the 3 foot zone in front of us.

Those who work in human services should be made aware of this fact. If you step into someone's personal environment, it has the same effect as violating their 3 foot personal zone. The person's anxiety increases even though you may be from 5 to 10 feet from the person.

▪ **Gender differences:** Gender differences also have an effect on a person's personal space. Generally, males are more territorial than females and have a larger personal zone. When a male approaches another male it is more threatening to both males than when a female approaches another female, or when a female approaches a male.

▪ **Personal habits:** People's personal habits can sometimes cause problems with regards to personal space. Some people get closer or touch as part of their upbringing which may have been in a warm family environment. They usually have very small personal zones.

On the other hand, research has shown that children who were not given adequate love or were raised in an environment of abuse (physical, emotional, or sexual) often become physically hostile as adults and have larger personal zones. If they are touched or their zone is violated by the person who is a "toucher," aggression can be quickly triggered.

▪ **Age:** Age is also a factor. As young children, our zones did not exist. For example, small children can walk up to and even touch adults, look up and say, "Hi," without reservations, but as we mature our zones begin to get larger.

Finally, studies have shown that personal

front – 3'
g ule 1'½'
lau 5'

space requirements are no different with individuals who were blind from birth. They also feel the pressure of having someone violate their personal space.

Reactionary Gap

As a general rule if we are within four feet of a person, and that person decides to punch, stab, kick, or disarm us, there is very little we can do about it. Within the four foot zone, their action will usually beat our reaction, or our **reaction time** will be slower.

Try this exercise: Stand two feet from your partner, both of you with your hands by your sides. Now quickly poke your partner with one of your index fingers in the stomach or on the tip of the chin. Your partner must try to stop the attack. Now try the exercise at three feet and again at four feet. As you get closer to the four-foot zone, your partner's reaction time gets better.

Imagine that finger being a knife or a punch. Within four feet of a potential aggressor is certainly not the safest place to be.

If a potential aggressor enters our personal space or if we have to enter their personal space, our hands should be at waist level or higher in a non-aggressive manner to reduce the time it takes us to react if an assault is attempted. A large percentage of personnel who are injured or disarmed do not understand the concept of space and reaction time.

Approaching Potential Aggressors

Before we approach potential aggressors we should have a mental plan of what we will do if violence occurs. What options do we have? What escape routes are available? What is in the environment that the aggressors can use against us? What can we use for our defense?

First, we should take three deep breaths which will increase our oxygen intake to relax us. When approaching potential aggressors, we should allow enough space to control them, but we should not violate their **personal space**. Standing 4 to 6 feet from them is generally comfortable for them and safer for us. For example, if we stop 8 feet away from the aggressors, we send a signal of fear. If we stop within 4 feet, we raise their anxiety level as well as our own and reduce our ability to react to an assault.

An approach can be made from two ways. One way is to approach the potential aggressors from the front and then blade your body 45 degrees relative to them. The other way is to approach them from a 45 degree angle (position 1 on Chart 1 in the Chart section) and then blade your body.

Imagine approaching potential aggressors and seeing a three-foot, oval shadow to your front which surrounds your entire body from your feet to the top of your head. A similar shadow is also in front of them. These shadows represent our **personal spaces**.

Therefore, your shadows will meet when you are 6 feet from the aggressors, and when you are 4 feet away they will overlap by two feet. However, if you are 4 feet from them and you blade or turn your body 45 degrees to the right or the left, the shadows will no longer overlap or meet. When you blade your body, it allows you to get closer to the aggressors without causing discomfort. Interlocking shadows means that there is pressure on you and the potential aggressors.

If possible, an approach should be made to

the weak side of the aggressors. This puts you further away from their dominant side and gives you
more time to react to an attempted assault. If you
are armed with a defensive tool, such as a gun, that
side should always be away and out of sight of the
potential aggressors. Your **vital line,** which is a line
running from your nose to your groin, should also
be protected and to the outside of the aggressors.

Some ways of identifying the potential aggressors' dominant or strong sides are:

■ Nine out of ten people are right handed

■ People gesture with their dominant hand

■ A watch is generally worn on the weak side

■ A belt end generally points to the weak
side

Another way to reduce the anxiety of potential aggressors, as well as to reduce the possibility
of an assault, is to approach them using the **supportive/defensive stance**. It is called the supportive/defensive stance because it is supportive or
non-aggressive to the other person and defensive
for you. This stance will put you on proper balance.

To get into this stance, your body should be
at a 45 degree angle relative to the potential aggressors. Your weak foot is forward and your
strong foot is to the rear. Your feet should be
shoulder width apart or wider. Your head should
be directly over your hips and your weight equal on
both feet with your knees slightly bent. The safest
distance is a minimum of 4 to 6 feet from the aggressors, depending on the stage of conflict
(discussed in Chapter 7). Whenever you are within
a 6 foot range of aggressors, both of your hands

should be at waist level or above in a non-aggressive manner.

Hand Positions

Some non-aggressive or supportive hand positions can be extremely defensive in the event of a potential attack.

- Place your hands at waist level with both palms up and open, and with one hand in the other hand. This is referred to as the "Father Murphy" hand position.

- Place your forearm furthest from the aggressor across your waist. Place your other forearm in a vertical position with the elbow on the wrist of the other forearm and your thumb under the chin with the index finger on your cheek. This is called "The Thinker" or "Jack Benny" position. Leaning your body slightly forward (by 5 degrees) indicates concern, but it also shows that you are not afraid. Leaning your body slightly backwards (by 5 degrees) indicates unconcern and fear.

Keep your hands off the potential aggressors. Do not startle, touch, poke, or pat. This may precipitate an assault.

Once again, approaches into private areas, such as bedrooms, offices, cars, hospital rooms, dorm rooms, or cells should be done with caution. Entering such areas has the same effect as entering a person's personal space.

Also, approaching potential aggressors who are down should be done from the side and not

from the top.   Imagine the three-foot, oval shadow
again.   When the aggressors are lying face up, the
oval shadow is in front of them from their feet to
the top of their head.

2

Eye Contact

Proper use of eye contact is an important non-verbal communications skill and you can use this skill to indicate concern, support, confidence, and authority to others.

We receive important messages from others by observing their eye movement when communicating with them. We can determine whether people are submissive, angry, deranged, under the influence of drugs or alcohol, looking for an escape route or weapon, or if an attack is imminent and where they might strike.

The length of eye contact during conversation varies among ethnic groups. On the average Caucasians maintain eye contact while speaking approximately 45% of the time, Blacks approximately 30%, Hispanics approximately 25%, and Asians approximately 18% of the time. In American society, **not** making eye contact gives the impression of insecurity, shyness, or deception.

Results of maintaining constant eye contact:

■ **Maintaining constant eye contact while we speak:** This can be interpreted as trying to dominate the other person which usually raises their anxiety level and is seen as an aggressive act. Decreasing eye contact reduces the power role and increases the helper (ally) role.

■ **Maintaining constant eye contact while we speak and we are taller than the other person:** This especially may be interpreted as an attempt at dominance.

■ **Maintaining constant eye contact while we speak and we are shorter than the other person:** This may be perceived as a sign of overconfidence or a challenge.

The opposite is true when the other person is speaking to us. Now, we want to maintain eye contact and gesture with small head nods or a slightly bowed head to show our support.

In review, to show our support when speaking to a person, we should periodically break eye contact with the person. Breaking eye contact can be as short as a 40th of a second, or the average time to blink an eye. To show support when the person is speaking to us, we should maintain eye contact and use head gestures.

■ **Direct, uninterrupted eye contact:** Might be used when we feel an assault is imminent or when we need to be assertive. Eyes that stare are very intimidating. Direct eye contact along with other body language signals and the use of defensive tools can sufficiently persuade aggressors to submit without a fight.

▓ **Wearing mirrored or dark glasses:** This acts as a constant, intense stare and is generally perceived as aggressive. Mirrored or dark glasses tend to hide the whites of the eyes which usually provide a constant source of information during conversation. These types of glasses take away the ability to see signals such as, darting eyes, jerking eyes, glazed stares, empty stares, look-through stares, and target glances. A person can only guess what is taking place behind the glasses. Also, different types of glasses have different effects. For example, heavy rimmed glasses have a tendency to make the wearer look more fierce and domineering. They also tend to make the wearer look as though they have a permanent, aggressive gaze, whereas wire rimmed glasses are usually perceived as non-aggressive.

What else can the eyes tell you? A great deal! The eyes are the dominant sense organs of the body. They are pathways to the mind that can tell us what the hands or feet will do before they do it.

After assessing the hands for any hidden weapons, your primary vision should be on the eyes and your secondary vision should be focused on body movements. Secondary vision allows you to view body movements when you are 4 to 6 feet away from a person.

Information relayed to the brain comes via the eyes by 87%, 9% comes via the ears, and 4% comes via the other senses. Your eyes are 1000 times more effective than the ears in sweeping information. For example, the eyes are efficient up to 1 mile and see light rays at frequencies of 10 million, billion cycles per second. They "are able to respond to one and a half-million simultaneous messages."3 Ears are efficient up to 100 feet and can hear frequencies of 50 to 15,000 cycles per minute.

The following are some examples of the importance of eye signals and what they can mean to us:

▣ Pupil Size:

Pupils cannot lie. The pupils of the eyes will dilate or contract as a person's attitude changes from positive to negative or vice versa.

When a person becomes excited, the pupils can dilate up to 4 times their normal size. When a person becomes angry, or there is intense hatred, the pupils contract. Contraction of the pupils is also known as "snake eyes" or "beady eyes."

▣ Alternating Eyes:

When a person's eyes are alternating from our eyes to our chest to our hands and back, it may indicate that they are sizing us up. We should maintain a proper distance and establish a good defensive position.

▣ Jerking Eyes:

This may indicate that the person is hallucinating. They may believe that they are communicating with God or Satan, with a non-existent friend or neighbor, or that they are being spied upon by an imaginary person. Create space and establish a good defensive position.

▣ Darting Eyes:

When a person's eyes are darting from

side to side or up and down, it may indicate agitation. Create space and establish a good defensive position.

▣ Looking Around Eyes:

This may be a sign that you have cornered the person and they may be looking for an escape route or weapon. Create space and establish a good defensive position.

▣ Glazed, Empty, or "Looking Through You" Eyes:

This may indicate one of several conditions, such as drugs, alcohol, medical problems, or etc. There exists here a higher potential for an aggressive act. The person may be inflamed with little or no provocation. Create space and establish a good defensive position.

▣ Target Glance or Look:

We are visual animals and we use our eyes for over 80 percent of our information. We look at the pen before we pick it up. We look at the paper before we write on it. We look at the basketball hoop before we shoot the ball. So, most people will look at a target before they attack it. A person probably will look at our chin before punching it, look at our groin before kicking it, look at our throat before cutting it, or look at our gun before grabbing it.

Knowing this gives us a tremendous advantage over the other person, especially since there is usually a pause of at least 4/10ths of a second between the glance (the time the person breaks direct eye contact, then looks at the target) and the attack. This pause gives us sufficient time to exit the attack zone (discussed in Chapter 16), or create space and verbalize.

■ Breaking Eye Contact:

A person uses direct eye contact and tries to intimidate us by yelling, screaming, or pointing a finger. This person will often break eye contact just before progressing to the next stage of conflict which is physical assault.

Depersonalizing us by looking down or away and then proceeding to look at the target just before attacking is common.

■ Widening Eyes:

Widening the eyes with the whites showing above and below the iris, is showing a basic response of surprise or fear. This will usually be followed by signs of submission.

■ Glistening Eyes:

Glistening eyes occur when the surfaces of the eyes are overloaded with secretion from the tear glands caused by aroused emotion, anguish, or distress. This is just one step short of crying.

A person may be constantly blinking in an attempt to get rid of the tears before they start crying. This is normally not a signal of danger to us, but rather a signal of a distressed person.

3

Gestures and Posture

In addition to understanding space and eye contact as non-verbal communications skills, there are numerous other ways that we continuously communicate with our gestures and posture.

If we say one thing, but send out a non-verbal signal that differs, the non-verbal signal will probably prevail. If a person says, "I give up," the appropriate body signals have to match the words. If there is a discrepancy between verbal and non-verbal signals, you should believe the non-verbal signals since they come from the subconscious and are therefore much harder to fake.

In the human services field, we cannot afford to rely on just one form of signal. We must look at several signals along with the rate, tone, and volume of speech.

There are many basic gestures and posture signals that we should be able to recognize and understand. Listed here are just a few. Note that each signal may be displayed by you or the other person.

Head

When the head is back, it shows aggression. When it is straight, it shows assertiveness. When the head is slightly bowed or nodding, it shows support or submission.

Face

When the face muscles show tension, or twitch or jerk, or when the teeth are clenched, the person is either showing signs of anxiety or aggression. Also, observe changes in skin color that may indicate rage, fear, or anger. Skin pales with rage or fear, and darkens with anger (in dark skinned individuals, there is no change in color).

When aggressors make the decision to attack, their faces distort more on the left side. Watch for more pronounced movement of the mouth on the left side of the face.

Lips

Quivering lips may be a sign of anxiety. When the lips are pushed forward bearing the teeth, it is a sign of anger. Tight or tense lips are usually a sign that an assault is imminent.

Breathing

The rate of breathing normally increases and gets deeper with aggression. A heaving chest may be a sign that an aggressor is about to attack.

Shoulders

Shoulders back usually indicates aggression. Shoulders straight may indicate assertiveness. Shoulders forward normally shows support or submission.

Arms

If the arms are crossed and high on the chest with closed fists and perhaps gripping the upper arms, this indicates aggression. If the arms are loosely crossed on the lower abdomen, this is usually non-aggressive.

Palms

- Above the waist, palms facing outward, this is non-aggressive

- Above the waist, palms facing inward, this is possible aggression

- Above the waist and bladed, this indicates aggression

- Below the waist, palms in, this is non-aggressive

- Below the waist, palms facing outward, elbows away from the body, this is non-aggressive

- Below the waist, palms facing outward, elbows close to the body, this indicates possible aggression

Hands

- Wringing hands indicate anxiety

- Opening and closing (pumping) of the hands show anxiety or aggression

- Hands on the hips indicate assertion

- Hands folded in front of the groin is non-aggressive

- Hands in the boxer stance indicate aggression

- Hands in the martial arts stance is aggressive

- Closed fists with white knuckles indicate aggression

- Hands close to the body, palms to the rear (open or closed) show possible aggression

- One hand open, one hand closed indicates a weapon is possibly hidden

■ One or both hands behind the back indicate a weapon is possibly hidden

Elbows

When the elbows are close to the body, this indicates tension, but if they are away from the body, this indicates a relaxed state.

Index Fingers

When someone points their index finger or simulates pulling a trigger with their index finger, or runs their finger across their throat in a cutting fashion, these are usually good signs of aggression.

Legs or Stance

■ When weight is equal on both feet, this is usually non-aggressive

■ When bobbing up and down on the balls of the feet, this usually indicates aggression

■ When rocking from toes to heels, this is usually aggressive

■ When the front knee is bent and the rear knee is locked, this is an aggressive sign

■ When they shift their body toward you, this is usually aggressive

■ When they shift their body away from you,

this may represent a threat, that they are looking for an escape or a weapon, or it may simply be a signal of submission

Note that an important signal used by martial artists is the shifting of their body weight. Usually individuals with martial arts backgrounds get into a stance by shifting 10% of their weight to the front and 90% to the rear, or 30% to the front and 70% to the rear.

Expanding the Body

Expanding the body, making it appear larger, is usually a sign of aggression, while contracting the body, making it appear smaller, is usually non-aggressive.

Leaning the Body

Leaning the entire body slightly forward, along with other support signals, increases the message of support. Leaning the body slightly backwards has the opposite effect, and indicates unconcern or fear.

Standing vs. Sitting

■ If we stand, and the potential aggressor sits, we are perceived as **more** aggressive

■ If we stand, and the potential aggressor stands, we are perceived as **less** aggressive

■ If we sit, and the potential aggressor sits,

we are perceived as the **least** aggressive

■ We should sit, blading our body 45 degrees and at least four feet from the potential aggressor in order to be perceived as supportive and to be safe from assault (see Approaching Potential Aggressors as discussed in Chapter 1).

Cornering

Almost every animal capable of self defense, from the smallest rodent on up, fights furiously when cornered with no means of escape. The most violent fighting behavior is motivated by fear or rage which can multiply the fighter's strength ten-fold.

Flight is often prevented by a lack of space, or by strong social ties, such as the defense of a friend or family member. "Fighting like a cornered rat" is often used to describe the desperate struggle that is motivated by fear.

We have a tendency to corner individuals, but we are often unaware that we are doing it. We frequently hear people say, "He went out of control for no reason at all." Often, the reason was that the aggressor was cornered and this triggered the aggression.

When cornering potential aggressors, we

leave them with one of three options:

1.) Resist
2.) Submit
3.) Flee

It is very difficult for you to verbally calm people down once they are cornered. Their focus is not on what you are saying, but on their space that you have violated. You must also realize that cornering potential aggressors increases your risk of injury. The following are common cornering mistakes:

Angular Cornering

Angular cornering is physically boxing the potential aggressor in a corner. In any situation where a potential aggressor has no avenue of escape, anxiety is increased.

The potential aggressor has only one option. Resist, submit, or flee by going through you in an attempt to escape.

Allowing the aggressor an avenue of escape by moving to one side and creating more space will lower the anxiety and reduce the possibility of a physical conflict.

Surround Cornering

Surround cornering is an attempt to show force by two or more people forming a semicircle around a potential aggressor against a wall. They can also completely surround the aggressor if the aggressor is out in the open and not against a wall. Either way, the potential aggressor has the option of resisting, submitting, or fleeing by going through one of the people.

Traditionally, teams of human service personnel have been trained to surround an aggressor as a show of force, to get compliance, or as a preliminary to control. In a team situation, each member of the team was assigned a limb to control.

This tactic has not worked and often violent confrontations occurred because the aggressors had the pressure of many people violating their **personal space** instead of just one. Injuries occurred because too many people were trying to control one aggressor. Also, the aggressors often took this situation as a personal challenge and became even more violent.

An approach should be made by only one person known as the contact person. The other team members should stay back at least 10 feet. Even though they are 10 feet away, they are still less than 3/4 of a second away from assisting the contact person. For example, if the potential aggressor has to be taken to the ground for control, it should be done only by the contact person through the use of proper techniques. However, another team member could be used as a distraction prior to the contact person making initial contact.

This tactic does not work and often violent confrontations occur. The aggressor has the pressure of many people violating their personal space instead of just one.

Contact Cornering

Contact cornering is the physical act of grabbing the potential aggressor. The aggressor is cornered in terms of limited choices and can either resist, submit, or flee.

Children who were not given adequate love or were raised in an environment of abuse often become physically hostile as adults and have larger personal zone requirements (discussed in Chapter 1 on Personal Space). Often aggression can be triggered simply by putting your hand on this type of person. A large majority of people who are incarcerated in correctional facilities fit this description.

Therefore, when you have to make contact, use the proper approach when entering their personal space and use the blanket or escort hold. It is always preferable to use gestures and verbalization skills to get potential aggressors to move from one location to another rather than to make physical contact with them.

In certain situations you may have to grab the potential aggressor before an attack on you or someone else is made. You must also be aware of the increased probability of a physical response.

Psychological Cornering

Psychological cornering is when you give someone a direct command. This forces potential aggressors to resist, submit, or flee. There is also less chance of compliance if their friends, family, or witnesses are nearby. Instead, give potential aggressors' options that will allow them to save face. For example, "Sir/Ma'am, please leave or **we** will have to . . ." versus "Sir/Ma'am, leave now!"

You should try to use **we** instead of **you** because **you** has a tendency to put people on the defensive (discussed in Chapter 5). "We will have to . . ." versus "You will be . . ."

A person who has become irrational needs to be given simple options that are enforceable.

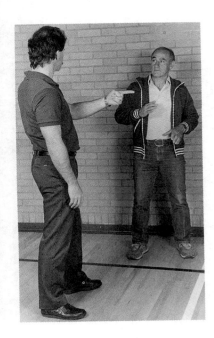

Direct commands force aggressors to resist, submit, or flee.

Exit Cornering

Exit cornering is the act of forcing a potential aggressor into your personal space. This usually occurs after you have diffused a potentially aggressive situation between two or more people. One person has submitted to your request to leave the area.

In one situation, you might position yourself by a door or open the door for a potential aggressor who has agreed to leave. This position forces the aggressor to be more submissive by entering your **personal space**. This act of submission, combined with your closeness, can also raise anxiety and re-ignite the aggression.

If you place yourself by the door, this position will force the aggressor to be more submissive by entering your personal space.

Another situation might arise when you force the aggressor to go between you and another person. This forces the aggressor to be more submissive by entering your personal space and the other person's. Aggression can also be reignited at this time and an attack may occur.

In both situations, you should move away from the aggressors and let them leave on their own terms. This allows them to save face and puts you in a better defensive position in the event violence occurs.

5

Verbal Communications Skills

We need to maintain a calm reassuring voice when communicating with people. We also need to communicate on their level, and paralanguage which is the way we say things, is very important. Whether we treat people as equals or as though they were inferior is reflected in our tone, volume, and rate of speech.

Most human services personnel are not trained to use verbal skills and agree that under stress they often shout commands out of frustration, not knowing how to handle the situation verbally. If we can resolve difficulties before they arise, then we can reduce the possibility of physical conflicts.

Common Verbal Communications Skills

Listed below are some common verbal communications skills that have been proven to be effective. They can be used individually or in combination with the others. Most of these verbal skills create and sustain conversation and the longer the length of conversation, the less the probability of a physical conflict.

- **Introduce Yourself:** Say, "Excuse me Sir/Ma'am, my name is . . . and I'm from . . . How can I help you?" This technique gets their attention and puts the focus on you. It also establishes who you are, your position, and sets the tone.

  This is a much better way of introducing yourself than asking first, "What's the problem here?" This puts the focus on them and the problem.

- **Ask Them to Repeat What They Said:** Say, "I'm sorry, but I didn't catch that. Would you please repeat what you said?" Ask them to repeat what they said whether you heard them the first time or not. This is part of active listening and shows that you care. Not only are you showing concern for them, but also your support.

  This technique reduces potential aggressor's anxiety and helps you to begin a conversation. It allows them to save face by rephrasing their statement and to hear what they said. This also gives you time to think, to formulate a plan, and to clarify the problem.

▦ **Ask Questions:** In a non-threatening and supportive manner ask, "I wonder if you could tell me . . .
- Who . . . ?
- What . . . ?
- When . . . ?
- Where . . . ?
- Why . . . ?
- How . . . ?"

Preface the above questions with, "I wonder . . . , I don't understand . . . , I need to know . . . ," or etc.

This also shows your concern, reduces anxiety, gets a conversation going, diverts their attention to talking about the problem, and gives you time to think and plan.

▦ **Repeat What They Have Said:** (Also called the "Reflection" or "Playback" technique.) "Joe/Mary, if I heard you correctly, you said . . . "

This shows your concern, indicates that you are listening, gets a conversation going, and gives you time to think and plan ahead.

Two exceptions to this technique would be threats of suicide or violence. You don't want to repeat the threats, but you do want to divert their thought processes.

▦ **Re-Direct Anger to the Past:** You do this by saying, "I feel that you were angry," or, "You became angry at them because . . . "

This technique causes them to think of their anger as having occurred in the past.

▦ **Interrupt by Using Their Names:** "Excuse

me, Joe/Mary." A person's **first name** is the single most important word in the dictionary.

Using their name puts them on your level and personalizes the encounter.

■ **Use "We:"**   When you use we, it indicates that what you say is not an order. It also indicates togetherness. Say, "Why don't we . . . ?"

We is the next most important word in the dictionary and using it puts you on the same level with them. It also reduces their anxiety which, in turn, increases your chances of compliance.

■ **Get Them to Sit With You:** Say, "I would feel better if we sat down." This relaxes numerous muscle groups and reduces their anxiety.

You should take the lead in sitting and use the proper seating arrangement of 4 to 6 feet away from each other at a 45 degree angle. At the same time, an offering of chewing gum, a cigarette, water, or coffee is a good technique to direct their thought processes to what you are doing and saying.

■ **Get Them to Walk With You:** Say, "Why don't we walk over to the . . . and get a cup of coffee." Walking reduces anxiety, expends energy, and removes them from their source of anger.

Removing them from another party who might reignite the aggression, or from a group of people where they feel they have to resist in order to save face is of great benefit.

■ **Use Pacing Techniques:** Pacing means setting an example, taking the lead, or getting in rhythm with someone. When you use "**I**" in pacing techniques, it transfers the focus of anger to you, the mediator. Examples of pacing are:
● **Sensory:** "I feel/I sense that you are upset with . . . "
● **Visual:** "I can see that you are upset with . . . "
● **Auditory:** "I hear/I understand exactly what you are saying."
These techniques provide feedback which is part of active listening.

■ **Use Voice Control:** Controlling your volume, tone, and rate of speech is critical and an important element of active listening.
   Approximately 10% of communication is verbal. Of that, 7% is what you say, 38% is how you say it, and 55% is your facial expressions as you say it.
   It is not what you say, but how you say it that is important. For example, if someone asks, "How was your day," you can answer "Great" meaning wonderful, or "Great" meaning disgusting. Your tone, volume, rate of speech, and facial expressions can indicate your enthusiasm or sarcasm.
   Also, the voice changes when someone lies. The rate and volume increases and the tone goes up most of the time. Examples would be someone saying rapidly and with increased volume, "Honest to God!" or "You may not believe this, but . . ."

- **Rate of Speech:** The rate of speech can show fear, lack of interest, honesty, authority, or support.
- **Tone:** Tone can indicate anger, resentment, meekness, assurance, support, or authority.
- **Volume**: Volume can show aggressiveness, meekness, support, or authority.

▓ **High-Risk Verbal Techniques:** These are not a good idea, regardless of whether they are used in jest or to try to add humor to a tense situation. Someone is usually offended or angered. Examples would be:
- "Look Shorty, Tubby, Four Eyes," or etc.
- "If I can't handle you, we have 10 more where I came from."
- To a Frenchman, "Hey Froggy, what's happening?"

Positive Commands

"An indispensable preliminary to battle is to attack the mind of the enemy."[3]

Under stress, people can only focus on a few action words. Using short, loud, positive voice commands takes their choices away. People are conditioned to obey positive commands. Saying, "Stop" gives them no choice. Saying, "Don't do it" gives them the choice to do it or not to do it.

Commands should be short and loud, and they should come from the diaphragm. Also, your body language should match the verbal dialogue. Examples of positive commands are:

- "Stop!"
- "No!"
- "Drop the chair!"
- "Look at me!"

▦ **Unbalancing the Mind:** When using positive commands, you are attacking and unbalancing the minds of the aggressors, causing fear and confusion. It's like turning their minds from one television channel to another.

    This in turn delays their planning process, giving you time to act. These commands may even break their morale and psychological will to fight (discussed in Chapter 12).

▦ **Ritualized Combat:** Positive commands can be used while aggressors are going through ritualized combat or intimidating rituals.

    An example would be: John is yelling at you with his fists clenched. You give a loud and positive voice command, "John, open your fists! Open your fists!" This redirects his thought process from what he is saying to his clinched fists.

▦ **An Assault is Imminent:** When aggressors are out of control and their body language tells you that an assault is imminent, positive commands can be extremely powerful defense tools. They attack the mind of the aggressors and force them to change their thought processes from what they intend to do to what they are hearing.

    Our minds are like computers; they are capable of focusing on only one thing at a time. For example, an aggressor raises a chair to strike you or another person. If you use a loud positive command, such as "Stop," it may cause enough of a hesitation to give you time to take action, such as to move away. One 4/10ths of a second delay will allow you time to move as much as 6 feet.

Holding Your Breath: During aggressive encounters, you may have a tendency to hold your breath, which quickly depletes your oxygen level. This may be why you are usually out of breath and feel weak in the legs after an encounter.

Loud, positive commands will not only force you to bring oxygen into your lungs, but it will change the aggressor's focus of attention from the aggression to what you are saying.

For example, an aggressor grabs you in a front choke hold. You should use multiple defense techniques while constantly bombarding the aggressor with loud positive commands, such as, "Stop...! No...!"

The confusion that you create in the mind of the aggressor will probably prevent the aggressor from focusing on the assault.

Continued Commands: When aggressors comply or hesitate with the first command, continue telling them what you want them to do next. Continued verbalization creates an intense state of inner conflict between aggression and fear, and reinforces commands.

Good examples are:
- "Stop . . . !"
- "Drop the chair . . . !"

- "Drop the chair . . . !"
- "Stop . . . , do it now . . . !"
- "Do it now . . . !"
- "Step away . . . !"

Used properly, positive commands can reduce the possibility of further and greater physical aggression.

6

Active Listening

$\mathbb{A}$ctive listening is defined as a system of opening and maintaining communications through the use of empathy, listening, paralanguage, and body language.

Empathy

Empathy is putting yourself in other people's shoes and really listening to their ideas or problems and waiting for their responses. Placing yourself in other's shoes will help you to understand what their problems are instead of prejudging.

You should try not to label or have negative prejudgments about people. Their problems are very real to them. They may show anger because they are feeling hurt, embarrassed, or frustrated. Empathizing with them will help you to identify and address problems in order to work toward solutions.

Listening

Listen to the ideas or problems of others because listening shows that you are concerned. Allow them to vent their anger or frustration. This will give you an indication of their level of anxiety or anger and helps you to determine if they are rational. This will also give you time to think and plan for a possible attack and to take three deep breaths to reduce your own anxiety.

It is very important to listen, but it can also be difficult to concentrate on what others are saying because we listen 3 times faster than we talk. We hear 400 words per minute and can speak up to 125 words per minute and because of this our minds tend to wander ahead of those who are speaking.

During one minute, our attention spans are effective for only 20 seconds. During the other 40 seconds, our minds are doing other things. It has been said that, "We only hear half of what is said; we listen to only half of that; and we remember only half of that."[4]

Wait for other's responses to determine the accuracy of the communications. Then respond in order to clarify. Never try to analyze what others are really feeling; rather try to ascertain what message is being conveyed.

When speaking to potential aggressors, avoid pointing your finger and using sentences that begin with "you." **You** is usually followed by should, "You should . . . "

Use the word "**I** rather than **you**" to begin your translation. "If I heard you correctly, what you said is . . . or, I'm sorry, I didn't catch that. Would you please repeat what you said?" You can put yourself in the other people's shoes but not in their minds. More important, don't ever try to set people straight.

Body Language and Paralanguage

Active listening also includes the use of body language and paralanguage. Paralanguage is how we say things and the volume, tone, and rate of speech we use.

It is important that we use proper body language as we listen to potential aggressors: eye contact, a head nod, a supportive/defensive stance, leaning slightly forward, a hand gesture, or etc.

By using the verbal skills discussed in the last chapter along with supportive body language, lower volume and tone, and slower speech we can reduce anxiety; the aggressors' and our own. The purpose of active listening is to open and maintain communications in order to resolve difficulties.

7

Stages of Conflict

There are three stages that people go through during conflict:

1.) Anxiety
2.) Losing Control Verbally
3.) Losing Control Physically

How to manage each of these stages will now be addressed.

Recognizing the Loss of Control

There are some very basic reasons why we, as a species, fight among ourselves:

■ To establish our dominance in a social hierarchy;   also known as the pecking order.

■ To establish our territorial rights over a piece of ground. For example, close males constantly strike each other in order to establish their masculinity.

■ In defense of our homes or extensions thereof. This only holds true for "normal" people. Abnormal people may fight, hurt, or kill others for pleasure, such as sadists, or they may perceive danger or threats that do not exist.

Also, "In our culture, 20 percent of people use aggression as their primary form of communications. It is not the last but the first tool used to express desires, needs, frustration, etc."[5]

Anxiety

In the first stage of conflict there is anxiety, a negative emotion. This is an involuntary reaction or response triggered by such things as:
- Fear
- Hate
- Frustration
- Disappointment
- Sorrow
- Jealousy
- Stress
- Guilt
- Paranoia

- Psychosis
- Distrust of authority
- Social or cultural factors (i.e. male confronts female authority figure)
- Someone cornered
- Someone crowded
- Someone in a foreign or uncomfortable environment
- Heat (over 200 years of research shows a relationship between high temperatures and aggressive behavior)

What happens to the body in the first stage? The autonomic nervous system consists of the sympathetic nervous system which prepares the body for violent activity and the parasympathetic nervous system which tries to restore the body to normal.

Along with the struggle of the autonomic nervous system, adrenalin is released into the bloodstream to prepare the body and mind for an emergency "fight or flight" situation. Listed below are a few of the many changes to the body caused by anxiety:

External Changes

- Face color becomes darker (in dark skinned individuals, there is no change in color) and facial muscles twitch and jerk
- Appearance of veins in the head, neck, and throat
- Lips twitch and are licked often
- Very little eye contact or staring
- Breathing is shallow and quickens; sighing
- Eyebrows are in a frown or twitch

- Sweating
- Head down
- Pacing or wiggling if seated
- Dryness of the mouth and tongue
- Clenched teeth
- Excessive swallowing
- Little verbalization or leaping from one subject to another
- Thickened speech or stuttering

Internal Changes

- Increased heart rate
- Increased blood pressure
- Increase in production of red corpuscles

Management

Our goal is to reduce the other person's anxiety by using the techniques discussed in active listening: empathy, paralanguage, and body language. The proper use of these techniques should calm most people down. However, there are always individuals who will move on to stage two, losing control verbally.

Losing Control Verbally

Losing control verbally occurs when people become verbally aggressive. They are defensive, belligerent, challenging, and they yell, scream, curse, or etc.

Generally, aggressors who are aroused to fight do not go into an all out attack for fear of injury. Aggression from the sympathetic nervous system drives them forward, but fear from the parasympathetic nervous system holds them back.

The aggressors begin by threatening to attack which is called "ritualized combat." If there is sufficient intimidation, their opponent backs off and the aggressors win without injury to themselves.

When threats and counterthreats fail to settle a dispute, an intense state of inner conflict arises and physical action occurs. Listed below are some of the external and internal changes that occur when losing control verbally:

External Changes

- Face darkens (in dark skinned individuals, there is no change in color)
- Lips push forward bearing the teeth
- Direct prolonged eye contact
- Quicker and deeper breathing
- Dryness of the mouth giving way to excessive salivation
- Eyebrows in a frown
- Head is back
- Shoulders are back
- Shoulders are squared to the opponent
- Standing as tall as possible
- Hands are pumping (opening and closing)
- Finger pointed and fist threatening
- Moving in and out of opponent's personal space
- Kicking the ground
- Shaking

Internal Changes

- Increased heart rate
- Increased adrenalin flow
- Increased blood pressure
- Increase in red corpuscles
- Stored carbohydrates rush from the liver and flood the blood with sugar
- Bladder and bowels may let go

Management

At this time, your goal is to get the aggressors back to stage 1, anxiety, and then to reduce the anxiety.

▪ **Non-Verbal:** Your body language should be assertive but not threatening. For example, stand in a good supportive/defensive position at least six feet from the aggressors. Lean slightly forward with palms out in a non-aggressive manner and maintain eye contact. This stance indicates that you are not afraid.

▪ **Verbal:** Allow the aggressors to vent for a reasonable period of time. Venting usually reduces internal pressure. If you don't allow them to vent, they may go to stage 3, losing control physically. Compare that to shaking a bottle of champagne and not allowing the pressure to be released by removing the cork. People who are not allowed to vent will often blow up.

Verbal communications should be assertive, not aggressive. You may also have

to give directions or set limits. These
directions or limits must be:
- Reasonable
- Enforceable
- Enforced

Otherwise, you will lose credibility and control later.

■ **Physical**: If two or more people are out of
control verbally, and it looks as though
physical aggression is imminent, you may
have to separate them (discussed in Chapter 22). At this stage, calling for assistance which is a show of force, may cause
them to calm down.

Sometimes you may have to use the
substitution technique. For example, you
personally may irritate the aggressors.
Perhaps you remind them of someone
they dislike.

Moving away from the aggressors and
allowing someone else to attempt to reduce their anxiety may be very effective. A
new face and a new approach, in other
words, a substitute. In some situations,
and for many different reasons, some aggressors will progress to stage 3.

Losing Control Physically

Aggressors begin losing control physically
when dialogue, or aggressive and countersignaling
have failed to settle the dispute. When this occurs,
the aggressors' physical signals are significant and

spontaneous.

It is critical that human services personnel understand and recognize these signals. Neglecting to do so will put them at a disadvantage and they can be seriously injured or killed. Listed below are some of the external and internal changes that may occur:

External Changes

- Face color pales (in dark skinned individuals, there is no change in color) and the blood quickly goes to the large muscle groups
- Distortion of the left side of the face will be more pronounced
- Lips will tighten over the teeth
- Aggressors break their direct stare, then look at their intended target (i.e. your chin, groin, gun, etc.)
- Eyebrows drop to cover and protect the eyes
- Head drops forward to protect the neck
- Verbalization stops. The focus of their brains is now on what they will do, and not on what they are saying.
- Breathing is rapid and deep to bring in more oxygen
- Stance goes from square shoulders to a bladed position. Usually the dominant side goes to the rear (i.e., getting ready for the John Wayne type punch).
- Body movement may stop
- They may rock back and forth from toes to heels or bob up and down on their toes
- If they are out of your reach, the final

signal of attack will be the lowering of their entire body or a quick dip before they go forward toward you (discussed in Chapter 14)

Internal Changes

- Heart rate is high
- Blood pressure is high
- Tunnel vision develops (vision narrows)
- Auditory exclusion occurs (you may have to use louder verbalization)
- Large amounts of adrenalin flow into the bloodstream

Management

When you see several or a cluster of these signals, assault is imminent, and you will have to take some type of action. Some options follow:

- Create space. Move away or put an object, such as a table or chair, between you and the aggressor.
- Use loud, positive commands (i.e., "Stop! No!") and an aggressive defensive stance.
- Aggressively draw a defensive tool, such as a capsicum aerosol spray (OC), a baton, or etc. Expandable batons, such as the PR-24® or the Cas Expandable have a tremendous psychological effect on preventing aggression.
- Divert the aggressor's attention with the use of an object (i.e., throw a handful of coins in the air, or drop a

clipboard, hat, keys, etc.).
- Move quickly into an escort position while verbalizing, or decentralize and take the aggressor to a prone control position (discussed in Chapter 18 and 20).

Submission

I f your countersignals are aggressive and fearful enough, the aggressor's parasympathetic nervous system will take over and the aggressor will back down or submit.

Signals of Submission

- Putting their hands up in front of their body with palms facing out
- Saying "I give up." This must be accompanied by the appropriate body language.
- Shaking hands
- Turning their back with their hands covering their head

- Reduction in violent movement, backing off
- Bowing their head
- Lowering their eyes; looking down; or widening their eyes
- Verbal tone and volume go down; rate slows
- Total inactivity; be aware of the danger if this occurs
- Falling to the ground; cowering, crouching; reducing body size
- Rubbing their hands; wiping off the sweat
- Pacing, or moving into your personal space
- Grooming gestures; adjusting clothing, hair, tie, or etc.
- Face may become pale (in dark skinned individuals, there is no change in color); a sign of fear
- Eyebrows lift and forehead wrinkles; a sign of fear or anxiety
- Eyebrows lower; a sign of anxiety

Re-Directed Activity

There are times when aggressors reach stage 3 and have to release aggression, regardless of how intimidating you are. They may release energy by striking someone else, kicking or punching a wall, throwing an object, etc. Thus, the aggression is released on a less intimidating object. This is common, but often misunderstood.

Confrontational Force Continuum

Along with an increase in violence and the number of assaults come an increase in civil claims and criminal allegations brought against human services personnel and their agencies. A large number of these lawsuits allege assault or excessive force on the part of the personnel. Many times the reports fail to provide complete information and leave the impression that force may have been excessive. Force is based on resistance and personnel must explain, not only the force, but the resistance also.

The confrontational force continuum starts with a non-aggressive situation and spans to a situation where personnel may be justified in using deadly force.   The actions of the aggressors are shown along with the personnel's non-verbal, verbal, and physical reaction options in Chart 2 in the Chart section.

The concept is designed to assist personnel in preparing their reports.   The reports must document the escalation of force based on the aggressors' actions and personnel/aggressor factors.

Factors such as organizational policies, state and federal laws, and court decisions regarding reasonable physical force and deadly physical force have to be taken into consideration.   We must be allowed to use a level of force higher than that of our aggressors, otherwise we would be in a no-win situation.   Also remember, as aggressors de-escalate their aggression, you must de-escalate the level of force you are using in response.

Personnel/Aggressor Factors

There are personnel/aggressor factors that may cause us to escalate quickly through the force continuum.   These factors may apply to us or to the aggressors.   These factors are:

- Age
- Size
- Gender
- Skill
- Disability
- Drugged
- Deranged
- Drunk
- Multiple aggressors
- Imminent danger

- Proximity to a firearm or weapon
- Ground defense
- Mode of assault

For example: A 50-year old, 140-pound female with a back disability is attacked by a 220-pound, 22-year old, male weight lifter on drugs. She has the right to use greater force than if a healthy 22-year old, 200-pound male is attacked by a 60-year old, 100-pound female.

Also, your special knowledge of the aggressors may also be factors which determine whether you should escalate quickly through the force continuum. Knowledge, such as:

- Frequency of past violence
- Seriousness of past violence
- Most recent incidence of violence
- Threats of violence
- History of substance abuse
- Clinical judgment about potential violence
- Amount of stress in the present situation

It cannot be stressed enough; if you do not put in your report information that is to your benefit, you may not be permitted to submit the additional information in court. It is crucial to write everything in your report.[6]

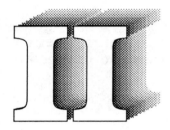

Personal Defense and Safety Skills

Introduction

A great many issues and options in dealing with aggressive individuals have been addressed in the last nine chapters which may effect the way you handle various situations. You may even disagree with some of the issues in these chapters. However, the main objective is to get you to think about various situations before they occur and the options you have to handle them.

We cannot accept what we know today about managing aggressive behavior as a guarantee or the last word on the subject. What we know today may be obsolete tomorrow. We must continue to learn better ways of handling aggressive individuals.

"Some experts think physical presence and communications skills alone could handle up to 98 percent of the incidents potentially requiring force."[1] However, proper training in non-verbal and verbal skills is essential. Without proper training in both of these areas your psychological techniques may precipitate aggression rather than reduce it. Therefore, there are times when meaningful interaction is not possible and you will have no choice but to intervene physically.

Many terms, such as "defensive tactics," "tactical defense," and "self defense" are used to describe methods of protecting yourself against different types of attacks. When attacked your goal is your own personal defense and safety, regardless of which of these terms you use.

If you can prevent an attack from occurring, both you and the attacker win. If you cannot prevent the attack from occurring, then you may be able to reduce the degree of force necessary to control the situation. The better trained you become the less force you should have to use.

Your life may be on the line, so know your limitations and use the various options accordingly. If you cannot reduce the degree of force necessary to control the situation, you may sustain an injury, but the key is to win the encounter. Remember, you must always be able to go home to your family, because you are not the aggressor.

There are basically two types of assaults; holds and strikes, and all assaults will fall in the hold or strike category. There are also two methods of assaults; static (stationary) and dynamic (moving).

In this section, we will examine assaults and the defense techniques that will work regardless of your strength or size. We will also look at alternatives to assaults. You will learn to use the appropriate technique based on the personnel/aggressor factors and the situation at the time of the assault.

10

Mental Conditioning

One area seriously lacking attention in personnel training is the area of mental conditioning. Professional athletes have practiced mental conditioning for years. At times, athletes hire mental health professionals to help them perform better under stress. Professional athletes understand that under stress they will resort to the techniques that they have practiced, whether they are physical or mental techniques.

The brain is like a computer, and if properly programmed, it responds accordingly. When suddenly faced with a dangerous situation, the brain stops conscious thought and shifts into automatic response mode. This automatic response mode is what moves your muscles without your conscious thought.

Information is brought up from the long term memory. If the brain has been properly programmed through mental conditioning, it responds with, "Oh yes, I expected this to happen and this is how I will handle it." If the brain was not programmed, nothing is brought up from long term memory and you will not respond, or you will respond too late.

Mental conditioning is as important as the practice of physical skills. It prepares you for a crisis before it happens. A key component is to make up your mind that a situation will occur.

You must practice what you will do before it happens. Repeated rehearsal, going over the situation again and again in your mind, in a safe setting improves your retention. This also gives you a sense of having been there before when the encounter occurs, and you will be better prepared for the encounter.

Clinical research and practical application have documented the effectiveness of mental conditioning. "Researchers found that imagining the movement also activated those same areas of the brain — with the exception of the motor cortex, which actually directs the muscles that produce the movement. In other words, mental rehearsal of an action puts the mind through a neutral workout that is not unlike that of the real thing."[7]

Mental Conditioning Exercises

These exercises only require a quiet place where you can relax.

▣ **Step 1: Relax.**
Relax in a comfortable chair, on a bed,

or on the floor. Breathe easily and think calmly.

▨ Step 2: Mental Imaging.

Imagine yourself confronted by an aggressor. The situation deteriorates to the point where you are attacked. See yourself reacting to the situation the way you were trained. Imagine yourself performing correctly.

▨ Step 3: Recover.

After mentally experiencing and handling the situation correctly, allow yourself to recover and relax.

▨ Step 4: Practice Imaging with Variables.

Add variables to your imaging exercises and use different scenarios. For example, have alternate plans A, B, and C. When the aggressor does this, then I will do this.

The single most important aspect of these mental preparation exercises is to see yourself performing correctly with the proper results. By so doing, you teach your mind and body that you can function effectively in these situations.

Proper Management Mind Set

What else is needed to insure that you are managing an aggressive situation successfully?

1.) Alertness

2.) Decisiveness
3.) Assertiveness
4.) Speed
5.) Relentlessness

Alertness

▨ Alertness can be described in three easy to remember levels; green, yellow, and red. Just like a traffic light.

- **Green — Unaware**. In this level you are unaware of your surroundings, as you are most of the time when you are driving a car. You are not consciously thinking about everything you are doing, like driving through several green lights without noticing that they are green.

- **Yellow — Caution**. In this level you are alert and know when something is wrong. It may be someone's body language or verbal signals. You are alert, but you have not made up your mind to do anything yet. This is similar to when you see a traffic light go from green to yellow as you approach.

- **Red — Take action.** In this level you have to take some form of action; yell, strike, block, retreat, shoot, or etc. Sounds easy enough, just do it, right? However, many people get injured or killed because they cannot take action or they take action too late. For example: Someone starts to show non-verbal and verbal signals of aggression.

You ignore them and remain in level green. When they go out of control, you may not be able to react fast enough to go from green — unaware, to yellow — alert, to red — take action.

The more mental repetitions you practice the greater the chance you will have of being successful.

Decisiveness

■ Since decisions take too long under stress, they should be made during mental conditioning exercises and in advance of the actual aggressive situations. There are many reasons why decisions are difficult to make under stress and some of the reasons have to do with fear. Some examples of fear include:

- Fear of being injured
- Fear of injuring someone else
- Fear of liability issues
- Fear of not complying with organizational policies

Assertiveness

■ When action has to be taken, you must be assertive and use 100% of your efforts, not 50%. For example, you strike an aggressor with your knee in the lateral femoral nerve center of the leg (see Chart 3 in the Chart section) in order to end a violent confrontation with only 50% of your force. This may only anger the aggressor instead of causing an interruption of the muscle groups to the lower leg. Consequently, you may have to use greater force with an increased potential for injury to both you and the aggressor.

Speed

■ Speed of thought and action, or automatic responses, come from mental conditioning. To simply ask yourself whether or not the aggressor is really going to hit you over the head with a raised chair is not speed of thought.

When you are justified, it is imperative that you take action before the aggressor does. Action always beats reaction. An understanding of imminent assault signals will help you act before the assault begins.

Relentlessness

■ You must be relentless in you efforts to stop an aggressor's assault on you. This may seem harsh, but it describes the mentality of conflict. It means you will do whatever it takes to win and survive, and that you won't give up if you experience pain. Those who mentally prepare for pain can handle it better and be less affected by it than those who don't.

Relentlessness must be short lived! It can not go on after the need for force is passed; otherwise it becomes brutality.

11

Myths and Assaults

Personal Defense Myths

When we think of personal defense we often think of martial arts such as Judo, Karate, and Kung Fu. We think of a time consuming effort on our part, and that we must be physically fit in order to be effective. We may also think that if we are small, female, old, weak, or disabled, that we cannot defend ourselves.

Think about teaching an eight-year old child how to ride a bicycle. Regardless of size, strength, or physical fitness, the child will probably learn in a few hours. Now, think about teaching the same child how to play classical music on a piano! Learning personal defense is equivalent to learning how to ride a bicycle, while learning martial arts is equivalent to learning how to play classical music.

Simple personal defense techniques are not complicated and do not take long to learn. To dramatize this point, visualize yourself small, weak, and confined to a wheelchair. A large male grabs you by the throat, picks you up and shoves you up against a wall. His face is six inches away from yours, and his grip is strong. You feel his thumbs pressing into both sides of your throat cutting off the blood supply to your brain. You begin to feel dizzy.

Now imagine placing the palms of your hands on each side of his head with your finger tips wrapped behind his ears. Bend your thumbs at the first knuckle and place the tips of your thumbs in front of his eyes. Now expel a loud "NO" as you drive the tips of your thumbs into his eyes as hard as you can.

You are small, weak, disabled, and untrained, yet you have just won a deadly force encounter, seemingly against all odds. You have defended yourself quickly with very little effort, and you have delivered an effective diversionary and release technique.

Types of Assaults

We will now address the most common types of assaults used by aggressors. Once you understand the options for defense against the holds and strikes in this book, you will be able to visualize and practice defenses against other holds and strikes.

Listed below are **types of assaults**:

▨ **Most Common:**
- Front choke
- Rear choke
- Punch (to the face)
- Club or knife (to the head)
- Kick (to the groin)

▨ **Common:**
- Side choke
- Bear hold (from the rear)
- Arm twist
- Weapon threat (to the front)

▨ **Least Common:**
- Full nelson
- Front bear hold
- Weapon threat (from the rear)

Personal Weapons for Defense

Personal weapons used for defense include:
- Head
- Thumbs
- Palms
- Heels of the palms
- Edges of the hands
- Backs of the fists
- Elbows
- Knees
- Shins
- Edges of the feet
- Heels

12

Assaults and Diversions

Focus of Attention

In assault situations aggressors can normally concentrate on only one thing at a time. Their focus of attention is on what they are saying (threats) or doing (physical acts). However, you have the ability to distract them quickly.

To illustrate this ability, practice the following: Have someone hold a rubber knife to your throat from the front. The person should say, "I want your wallet and if you resist I'll hurt you." While they are threatening you, grab the hand holding the knife and move it to the side. You will notice that verbalization immediately stops when you grab the person's hand. The focus of attention is quickly diverted from what they are saying to what you are doing.

Physiological Diversions

Physiological diversions act directly on one or more of the aggressor's five senses. A physiological diversion causes confusion and disorientation, and tends to heighten the aggressor's fear. This fear, in turn, may lead to the aggressor's submission, so watch for the signals.

Physiological responses are involuntary and cause the aggressor to focus on something else which gives you time to react. For example, a one-half second distraction provides you with enough time to move approximately seven feet away, to strike, or to decentralize the aggressor.

Some examples of diversions are:

- A loud command, such as "Stop!" or "No!"

- A loud blast from a whistle

- A hand gesture (Stop)

- An object thrown at the aggressor's face or feet (i.e., keys, a clipboard, a hat, or a wallet)

■ A strike to a vulnerable area on the body

■ An escape technique:
   ● Moving behind an aggressor from an escort position
   ● Side stepping as the aggressor lunges

13

Defense Against Holds

$\mathbb{B}$ efore performing any defense technique, you should lower your center and get into a good supportive/defensive position. It will then be more difficult for an aggressor to push you off balance or to the ground.

Verbalization should be used while you free yourself from the aggressor. Once the release is made, you should control the aggressor or create distance, and verbalize.

Your defense options are determined by the actions of the aggressor. In any situation requiring the use of force, you must assess the level of threat and determine the appropriate level of response. Remember that deadly force is defined as any force that is likely to cause serious physical injury or death.

Deadly force may never be used in defense of property. You can only respond with deadly force when you have determined that the threat level is likely to result in serious physical injury or death. Then, any force is acceptable that will deter the attack if it does not unreasonably endanger other individuals who may be present.

Before using force which is likely to result in serious physical injury or death you must have a reasonable belief that the aggressor intends to do great bodily harm to you. To assist you with that determination, evaluate whether the aggressor has demonstrated an intent to harm you and has the ability to do so.

Response Options

Begin by stabilizing yourself and verbalize with words such as "No" or "Stop."

Attempting to release a hold is recommended when you perceive that there is a reasonable probability of success, or as a follow-up to a response which has weakened or distracted the aggressor.

Front Choke

To make an aggressor release a front choke any of the following **eight options** demonstrated can be used with personal weapons, such as your head, thumbs, or palms:

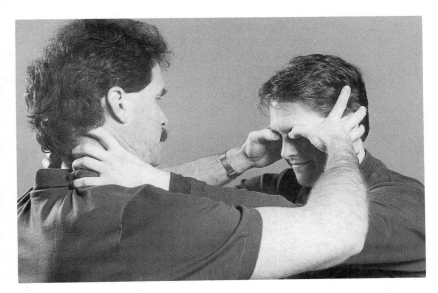

Option 1: Place your fingers behind the ears and compress the aggressor's eyes with the tips of your thumbs.

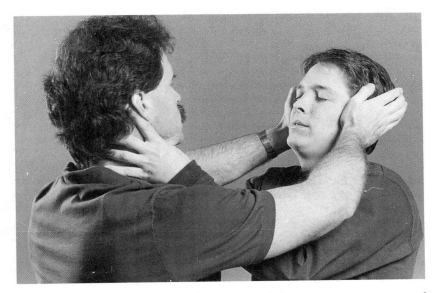

Option 2: Strike the aggressor's ears with the palms of your hands.

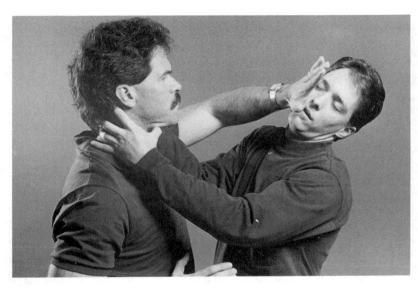

Option 3: Strike the cheek or nose of the aggressor with the heel of your palm.

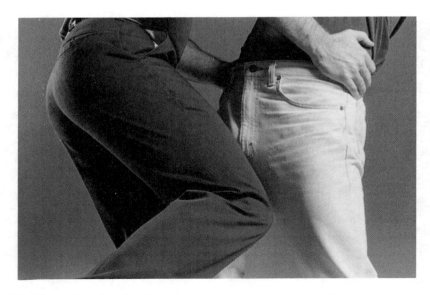

Option 4: Grab the aggressor's head, neck, arm, waist, or belt and strike the groin with your knee.

Option 5: Grab the aggressor's head, neck, arm, waist, or belt and strike upwards into the groin with your shin.

Option 6: Push up with your strong hand on the aggressor's elbow opposite your strong side.

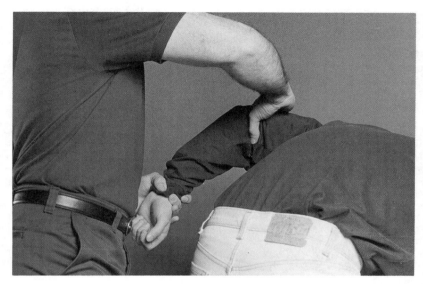

Simultaneously grab the aggressor's strong wrist with your weak hand, palm out, and go into an escort position.

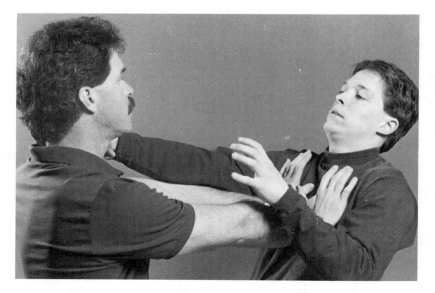

Option 7: Push against the aggressor's chest with both of your hands while yelling "No!" or "Stop!"

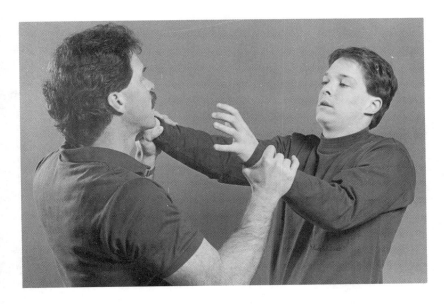

Option 8: Grab the aggressor's wrists and push away.

Side Choke

The following **three** options shows how to make an aggressor release you from a side choke.

Option 1: (Bottom photo on previous page) **Strike the aggressor's cheek or nose with the heel of your palm, or strike the groin in an upward movement with the ridge (thumb side) of your hand from the front or rear.**

Option 2: Strike the top of the aggressor's instep with the inside edge of your foot. At the same time grab the aggressor to stabilize yourself.

Option 3: Place your thumb closest to the aggressor in the aggressor's armpit from behind and grab the aggressor's wrist with your other hand.

Simultaneously strike the aggressor's ribs with your chin and pull the aggressor's arm away from your neck. Once the release is complete, go into the escort position.

Rear Choke

To make an aggressor release a rear choke any of the following **five options** demonstrated can be used.

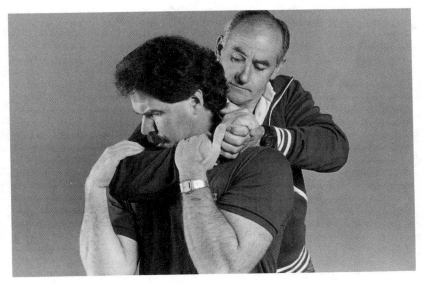

Option 1: Protect your airway by grabbing the aggressor's elbow with one hand and the aggressor's wrist with your other hand. Pull both of your hands down and toward your center, and tuck your chin into the aggressor's elbow.

Option 2: (Top photo on following page) Release your hand from the aggressor's wrist. While maintaining a downward pull on the aggressor's elbow, find and strike the aggressor's groin with the edge of your hand.

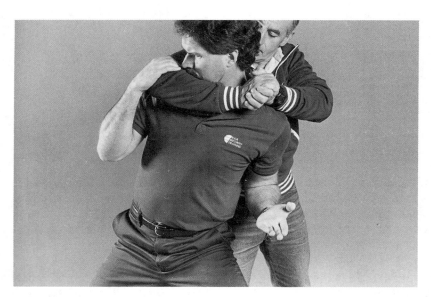

Option 3: Strike the aggressor's ribs with your free elbow.

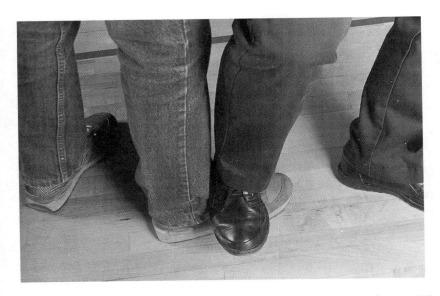

Option 4: Strike the top of the aggressor's instep with your heel or the edge of your foot.

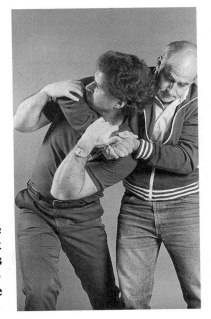

Option 5: Step behind the aggressor with your foot that is closest to the aggressor's hand. Place your thumb closest to the aggressor in the aggressor's armpit.

Grab the aggressor's wrist with your other hand while simultaneously striking the aggressor's ribs with your chin and pull the aggressor's arm away from your neck. Once the release is complete, go into the escort position.

Bear Hold

The following **four options** demonstrate how to make an aggressor release you from a bear hold.

Option 1: Move your hips to either side and strike the groin with the edge of your hand.

Option 2: Strike the aggressor's face with your head.

Option 3: Strike the top of the aggressor's instep with the outside edge of your foot or with your heel.

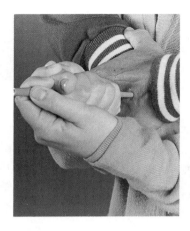

Option 4: Pull hard on one of the aggressor's fingers, or press an object, such as a key, pen, thumb, knuckle, or etc., into the back of the aggressor's hand.

Arm Twist

To make an aggressor release an arm twist any of the following **three options** demonstrated can be used:

Option 1: Turn in the opposite direction of the twist to ease the pain on your arm.

Strike the aggressor's face with your free elbow.

Option 2: Strike the aggressor's head with your free fist.

Option 3: With your free arm hook the aggressor's wrists in the crook of your elbow and squeeze hard. While maintaining control of the aggressor's wrists with your elbow, jerk your caught arm free.

Techniques used in the above situations can be applied to most other holds. Visualize other situations. What are your options?

14

Stationary Defense Options

If you are four to six feet from an aggressor you will usually have time to exit the attack zone. If there is no time and you are stationary (static) and you have observed the non-verbal signals of imminent assault, move into a supportive/defensive stance.

To avoid personal injury you should take every opportunity to avoid the necessity of having to block using your arm. Sometimes, however, you may have no other options available to you. In such situations, the following defense techniques may prevent you from being seriously injured.

A Club, Edged Weapon, or Punch to the Head

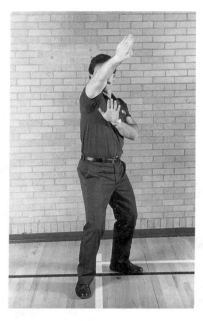

From the supportive/defensive stance, raise your arm closest to the aggressor. Also keep your strong side to the rear if you are armed.

Hold your arm up diagonally between your eyes and the aggressor's. Your elbow should be locked and your palm toward the aggressor.

Yell "Stop" prior to the attack to divert the aggressor. Also a yell of "Stop" at the time of the attack may reduce the force of the attack.

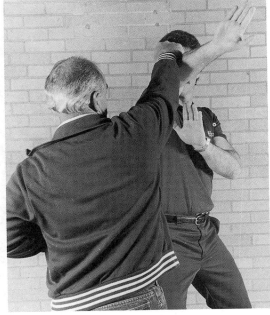

Once the attack is deflected, you should have a mental plan to escape, to strike, or to control the aggressor.

A Kick to the Groin

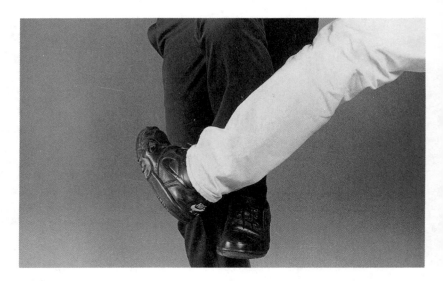

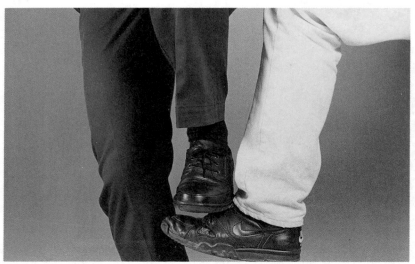

From the supportive/defensive stance, raise the knee closest to the aggressor across your body, keeping the foot flat and parallel to the ground. This will block a front kick (top photo) or a round-house kick (bottom photo) to the groin.

Keeping your eyes on the aggressor will give you time to escape when the aggressor looks down.

Once the attack is defeated, you should have a mental plan to escape, to strike, or to control the aggressor.

An Armed Threat From the Front

The following **two options** can be used for any frontal threat involving a gun, edged weapon, club, or etc.   These options are appropriate whether the threat is at face, chest, or stomach level, and whether the threat is in one or both of the aggressor's hands. Also, execute these techniques while the aggressor is talking to you, or while you are talking to the aggressor. Two principles apply here:

- ▓ Action beats reaction within the reactionary gap of four feet.

- ▓ Focus of attention; the aggressor can only focus on one thing at a time, the threat or the verbalization.

Option 1: Pivot your upper body sideways and grab the largest part of the aggressor's hand. Your thumb should be under the aggressor's hand and your fingers over the hand.

The preferred block should be performed so that the aggressor's arm is across the aggressor's body. Proceed to strike the aggressor's nose with the heel of your palm. The elbow of your blocking arm should be locked.

Option 2: Strike the aggressor's groin with your knee.

        Continue repeated strikes while verbalizing until the threat is eliminated. You should also have a mental plan that includes your escape, or the disabling and control of the aggressor.
        During armed attacks disarming techniques may lead to the following events, so precautions should be taken to eliminate them:

   ▧ An accidental weapon discharge

   ▧ The escalation of aggression by the
      aggressor

        The following factors should also be taken into consideration:

   ▧ Level of threat

   ▧ Bystanders

   ▧ Personnel/aggressor factors

An Edged Weapon Attack From the Rear

        It is suggested that you execute these techniques while the aggressor is talking to you, or while you are talking to the aggressor. The aggressor can only focus on one thing at a time, the threat or the verbalization. Also you should have a mental plan that includes your escape, or the disabling and control of the aggressor.

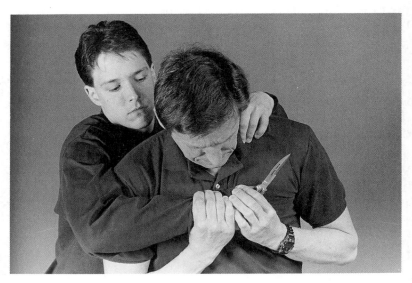

Option 1: Grab the aggressor's wrist with one of your hands and the aggressor's hand with your other hand. Pull the aggressor's weapon hand down into the center of your chest. Turn toward the weapon hand and keep the weapon tight to the center of your body.

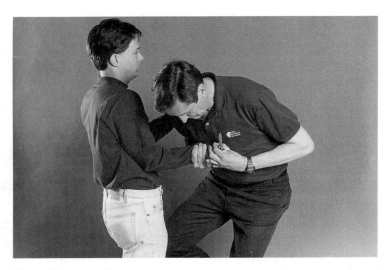

Option 2: Strike the aggressor's groin or body with your knee while verbalizing.

Option 3: Strike the aggressor's nose with the heel of your hand. Continue repeating strikes until the threat is eliminated.

An Edged Weapon Attack (in a Jabbing, Slicing, or Tapping Manner)

You are confronted with an aggressor who is using an edged weapon in a jabbing, slicing, or tapping manner. It is best to create space between the aggressor and you, or to get a barrier between the two of you.

Verbalize with loud, positive commands which may direct the focus of the aggressor's attention away from the attack.

If there is no room to move, or no time to get a weapon, and the assault is imminent, drop to the ground with your feet between the weapon and your head.

This will:

- Act as a diversion

- Put greater space between your neck and the weapon

- Give you time to plan.

The following options should also be used if you slip, trip, or are knocked to the ground:

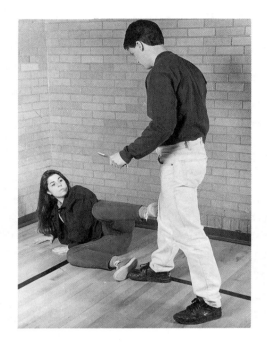

Option 1: Lie on your side with both hands on the ground and both feet tucked in. Strike the aggressor's lower knee or shin with the bottom of your foot.

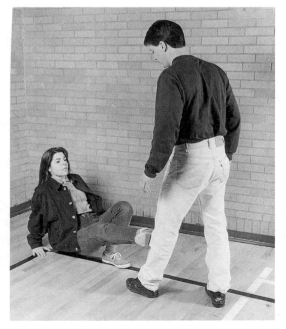

Option 2: While in a seated position, place your hands on the ground next to your hips. Push up on your hands and extend one leg towards the aggressor.

Strike the aggressor's lower knee or shin with the bottom of your foot. Make sure that your striking foot is parallel to the ground with your toes pointing out.

Option 3: Lie on your back with one knee bent and your foot on the ground. Your other leg should be straight with your toes pointing out. Now strike the aggressor's knee or shin with the bottom of the foot of your straight leg.

This is a better option against multiple aggressors, or if you carry a great deal of equipment on your belt.

A Thrown Object

You are down and an aggressor intends to throw an object at you.

Roll onto your back and raise both legs. Your knees should be bent and the bottom of your feet between the object and your face.

Your feet will absorb the force of the object. Also keep both arms raised, palms out, between the object and your face as additional protection.

Getting Up Safely

When human services personnel are down and aggressors are up, it is common for personnel to suffer injuries from kicks to the face and ribs when they try to get up. The act of getting up may only take you two seconds, but an aggressor who is eight feet away can attack you in less than one second.

You should only try to get up if the aggressor is disabled or you feel you can get up safely.

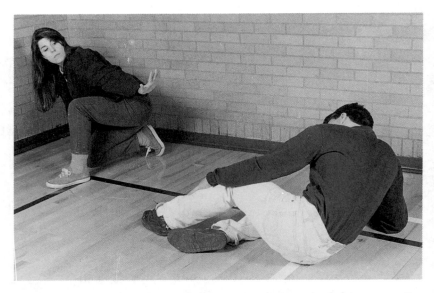

Kneel on one knee and bring the other knee up so the ball of the foot is flat on the ground. For support, one hand is on the ground and the other hand is between the aggressor and you in a defensive position.

Keep your body perpendicular to the aggressor and push off with the foot closest to the threat. Then move away from the aggressor.

Stand up into a defensive position. If on the way up you are attacked, you can go down into a good defensive position again.

15

Methods of Moving

During physical encounters human services personnel often find themselves on rough terrain, ice, slippery surfaces, or in cluttered areas. When moving in self defense they often trip, slip, or are thrown down.

Proper methods of movement can often eliminate going to the ground. The forward and rear shuffles are effective when moving straight or diagonally. The lateral shuffles are effective in lateral or circular movements.

Forward Shuffle

From the defensive position push forward off your strong foot and slide your weak foot forward a comfortable distance.

Slide your strong foot forward the same distance. You will end up in virtually the same stance as before, only further forward.

You will end up in virtually the same stance as before, only further forward.

Rear Shuffle

From the defensive position push backwards off the weak foot and slide your strong foot back a comfortable distance. Slide your weak foot back the same distance. You will end up in virtually the same stance as before, only further backwards.

Lateral Shuffle (Strong Side)

From the defensive position push off your weak foot towards your strong side. Now slide your strong foot laterally a comfortable distance towards the strong side. Slide your weak foot laterally towards your strong side the same distance. You will end up in virtually the same stance as before.

Lateral Shuffle (Weak Side)

From the defensive position push off your strong foot towards your weak side. Slide your weak foot laterally a comfortable distance towards your weak side.

Slide your strong foot laterally towards your weak side the same distance. Once again, you will end up in virtually the same stance as before.

16

Moving Defense Options

$\mathbb{T}$he Tueller Drill shows that an aggressor, armed with a knife, can close a 21-foot distance and deliver a fatal thrust in 1.5 seconds.

If an aggressor attacks from say 6, 10, or 20 feet, you will have a high potential for injury if you:

- Try to draw a defensive weapon such as OC spray, baton, gun, or etc.

- Attempt to go backwards

■ Stand your ground

The obvious thing for you to do is to exit the attack zone using the one of the following options:

Option 1: Use a lateral shuffle to the aggressor's weapon side, if possible.

In moving to the aggressor's weapon side, you reduce the strength of the attack. The reason for this is that while in motion, the aggressor is striking away from the center line of the body.

In moving to the aggressor's non-weapon side, the strike would be coming across the aggressor's body and in line with the body's center line. This gives the aggressor more strength.

Option 2: Move to the rear of the aggressor and as far away as possible.

Option 3: Verbalize with positive commands from an aggressive/defensive stance.

Draw a defensive tool, if you have one, or place an object between the aggressor and you.

If you have no escape route, go into a ground defense position using the options previously discussed in Chapter 14.

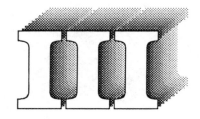

Physical Control Techniques

Introduction

No one physical control technique is effective 100% of the time against all aggressors you may encounter. If you master a technique, you can reasonably expect it to work to establish control in most situations. However, there are times when control techniques will not work and alternative measures will have to be used.

In order to apply a physical control, joint manipulation, or joint compression technique, you must have:

- Compliance by the aggressor

- Diverted the aggressor's focus of attention

- The ability to overpower the aggressor

Stay flexible. You do not have to make one technique work. You have the option of:

- Disengaging

- Using other options going up or down the confrontational force continuum

If an aggressor stops resisting, then the use of force **must also stop**. Use "if/then" thinking. If the aggressor does this, then you will do that. Also, have alternate plans of action.

In this section, we will look at how to approach safely, escort, decentralize, direct to a prone position, control, and separate aggressors.

17

The Blanket Hold

When you touch or grab aggressors you have:

- ▓ Entered their personal zone which increases their anxiety

- ▓ Greatly reduced your ability to react

- ▓ Cornered them which leaves them with the decision to either resist, flee, or submit

The blanket hold represents the lowest amount of threat to the aggressor because of its soft, non-threatening, fingertip touch. Applying the hold at the elbow is easier than grabbing the wrist because the elbow is less mobile and can only be moved half as fast as the wrist.

To apply a blanket hold, simultaneously place your hands lightly on either side of the aggressor's elbow as you verbalize using a low tone and volume.

Try using the fingertips only. One hand goes in front and the other hand goes behind the elbow with your thumbs up. The aggressor cannot elbow or backhand you.

This is a gentle hold, yet it provides surprising control. The blanket hold gives you the ability to move into the escort position or to use other defense and control techniques.

18

The Escort Position

From the blanket hold, while verbalizing, slide the hand that is in front of the elbow down and lightly grab the aggressor's wrist. Keep your thumb to the inside of the wrist.

The aggressor's arm should be at a 45 degree angle away from you and the hand facing to the rear. Keep the aggressor's elbow from bending which greatly reduces the strength in the arm.

The fingers of your other hand should be wrapped lightly around the inside of the aggressor's elbow with your thumb to the outside. The elbow should be at your center with your shoulder behind the aggressor's shoulder.

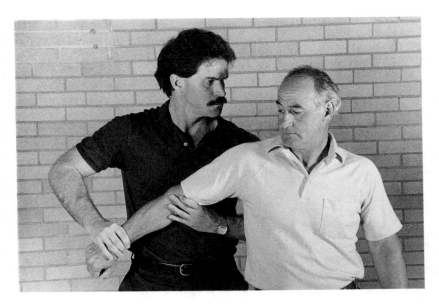

The escort position is performed 45 degrees to the rear of the aggressor.

This is also the 2 1/2 position of approach on Chart 1 in the Chart section. From this angle you have the advantage of leverage and it becomes harder for the aggressor to kick, grab, or punch you.

From the escort position you have numerous options if the aggressor becomes resistive. You can disengage and escape, escort, or decentralize and direct to a prone position.

19

Entering the Personal Zone

Entering the personal zone of every individual to apply a blanket or escort hold is not appropriate. It is appropriate for passive or passive-resistive individuals, but not for those who are actively resisting or assaulting you.

Also, placing your hands on individuals is only appropriate when you have the lawful authority to physically remove them from a location. Otherwise, such actions may constitute tortious conduct on your part which is the same as assault or battery.

Passive Individuals

Keep your hands in a non-threatening gesture while you maintain eye contact and verbalize.

Approach from a 45 degree angle. This makes you appear to be invading less of the individual's personal space. Your vulnerable line should be facing away and to the outside of the individual. If you are armed with a defensive tool it should be away from the individual.

Use the supportive/defensive stance and approach with a forward shuffle.

Never walk straight into the reactionary gap. This exposes your vulnerable line and you will be off balance as you step forward.

Make initial contact with the blanket hold.

Guide and escort the individual from the 2 1/2 position (see Chart 1 in the Chart section).

Passive-Resistive Individuals

Approach from a 45 degree angle while maintaining eye contact and verbalizing. Keep your hands up in a non-threatening gesture.

Use the supportive/defensive stance and enter the personal zone quickly with a forward shuffle. Carry out your plan of action decisively.

Make initial contact with the blanket hold. If the individual's arm is moving, make contact on the upper arm near the shoulder; then slide your hands down to the individual's elbow.

Quickly pivot into the escort position. Most people get hurt by hesitating in the middle of a plan of action.

Individuals Attempt to Escape

The individual you have in the escort position or the blanket hold may become violent and attempt to strike or grab you. However, remember that your use of force can only escalate in response to the aggression. That is, your use of force must appropriately increase equally to the individual's actions.

You can control the individual without injury if you use an OC (oleoresin capsicum) product or a lateral vascular neck restraint.

If you do not have your OC spray handy or you can't readily get into a position to use the lateral vascular neck restraint, use one of the following options to protect yourself:

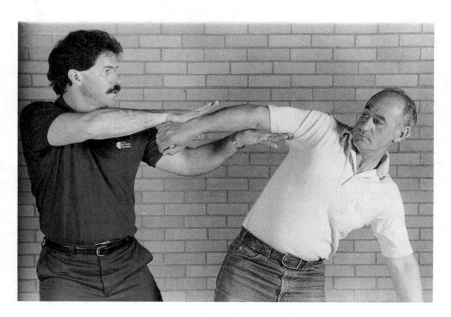

Option 1: Push the aggressor away from you and rear shuffle into a defensive position.

Option 2: Pull the aggressor across your body and use the momentum created to take the aggressor off balance. Lateral shuffle behind the aggressor and go into a defensive position.

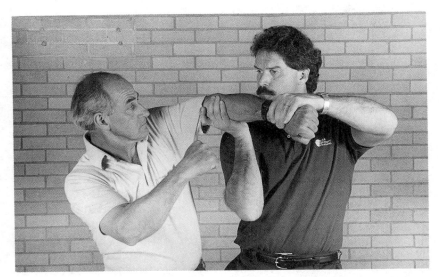

Option 3: Use a verbal diversion, such as "Stop" or "No," and raise the aggressor's elbow.

Strike the aggressor's face with your hand that was holding the aggressor's wrist or use the heel of your palm. This also protects your face from a strike by placing your forearm diagonally across the line of attack.

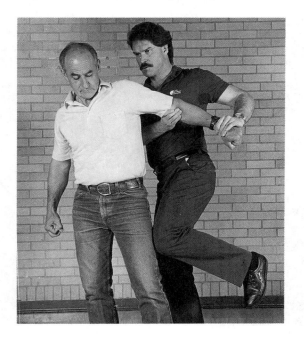

Option 4: Strike the lateral femoral nerve center with your knee that is farthest from the aggressor (Chart 3 in the Chart section).

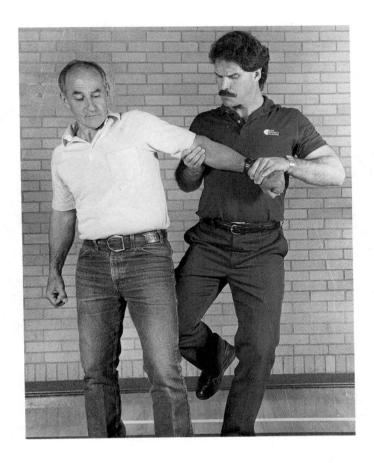

Option 5: Use a knee strike to the common peroneal nerve center with your knee closest to the aggressor (see Chart 3 in the Chart section).

Impact to leg nerve centers is an excellent way to partially disable **aggressors** who are under the influence of drugs or alcohol, or those who are emotionally disturbed and do not feel pain. It is one of a few ways to control them without inflicting serious injury.

Escort Techniques From the Escort Position

Non-Resistive Individuals: Use the escort position to escort individuals. Maintain eye contact and verbalize.

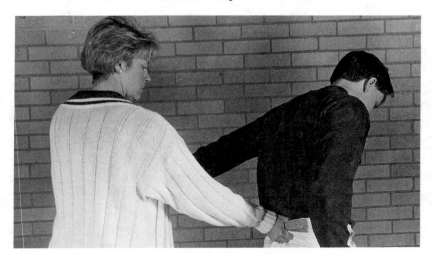

Semi-Resistive Individuals: Use the wrist/small of back escort.

Release your hand at the individual's elbow and grab the pants, belt, or clothing at the small of the individual's back with your thumb down and fingers up. Escort forward or rotate the individual in the direction of resistance and verbalize.

Use this technique for moving a resistive individual through a doorway, but rotate the individual 180 degrees before going through the doorway.

Resistive Individuals: Low level, pain compliance techniques are appropriate when holding an individual for arrest, for an individual who is under arrest and resistive, or to prevent violence by the individual. There must always be justification for the application of pain.

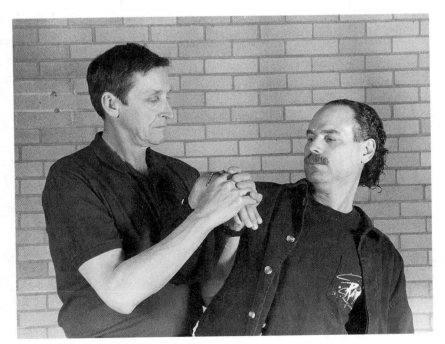

Option 1: Apply a rear bent-wrist compression.

The individual's elbow is in the center line of your body and the individual's forearm is at a 45 degree angle. Pressure is applied with your middle finger which is just above and in line with the individual's knuckles.

Escort the individual as you walk forward and verbalize. Reduce pressure when the individual complies.

This technique combines leverage and pain to your advantage. It also keeps the individual off balance and you on balance.

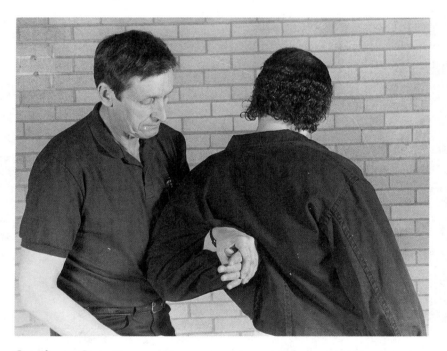

Option 2: From the escort position, push the individual's hand behind the back as you pull the individual's elbow into your center.

Rotate your hand on the top of the individual's hand. Your middle finger is just above and in line with the individual's knuckles and your fingers are pointing downward. The individual's fingers are pointing to the rear and away from the body.

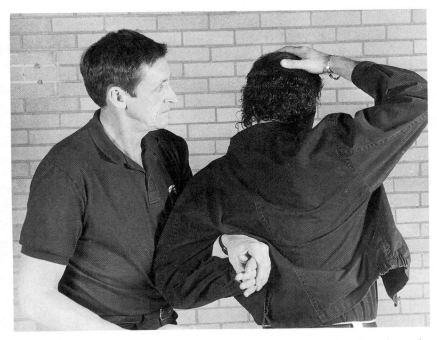

The individual's other hand should be on the head. Escort the individual as you walk forward and verbalize. Reduce pressure when the individual complies.

20

Decentralization Techniques

Decentralization or to "take off balance" means to get an aggressor's head out of line with the hips. Aggressors who are off balance have less ability to resist than those who are on balance.

Decentralization techniques can be done with or without diversions. However, the technique is usually more effective after a verbal command or a physical diversion is used.

From the Escort Position

Wrist Pull: Pull the aggressor's wrist and elbow simultaneously downward at a 45 degree angle and across your body. This takes the aggressor off balance.

This technique can also be accomplished from the blanket hold by pulling downward on the aggressor's elbow at a 45 degree angle.

Bent Elbow Push: Push upward and then forward with the heel of your palm on the bent elbow, taking the aggressor off balance (see top photo on the next page).

Keep the aggressor's wrist and elbow in line with your center and keep a 90 degree bend to the aggressor's elbow.

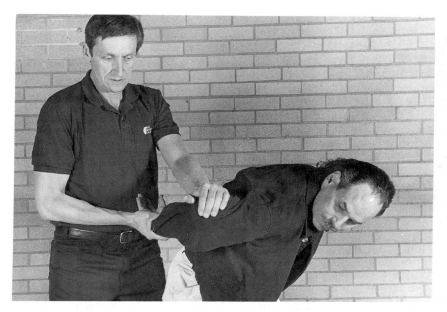

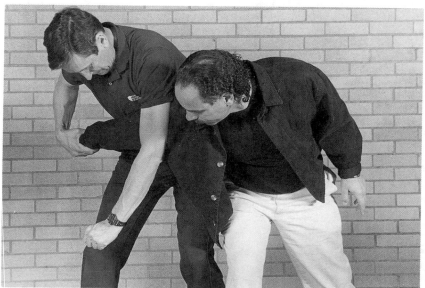

Forward Bend: Place the aggressor's elbow in your center and your arm over the aggressor's biceps. Bend forward over the aggressor's elbow. Keep the elbow in line with your center and apply pressure to the biceps.

21

Directing to
a Prone
Position

When the aggressor is decentralized, direct the aggressor to a prone position. Verbalize continuously as you apply the following techniques:

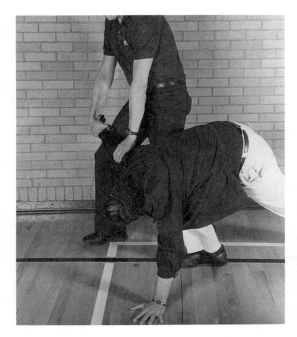

From the Wrist Pull: Place the aggressor's wrist just above your knee. Lock the arm that is controlling the aggressor's elbow and apply downward pressure.

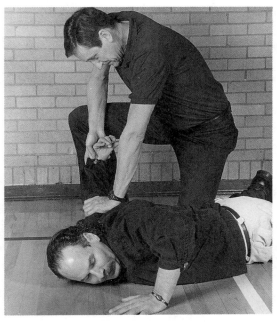

Once the aggressor is prone, use a control technique.

From the Bent Elbow Push: Keep the aggressor's wrist in line with your center and push straight down on the aggressor's bent elbow.

Your arm should remain locked for leverage and keep a 90 degree bend to the aggressor's elbow. Once the aggressor is prone, use a control technique.

From the Forward Bend: Kneel down and keep your weight on the aggressor's arm.

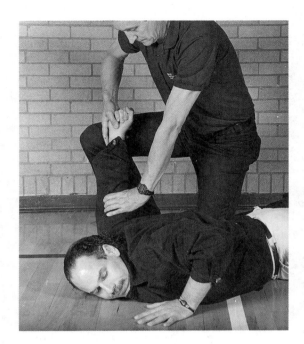

Make sure the aggressor's arm stays locked with the palm of the hand toward the rear. Once the aggressor is in a prone position, use a control technique.

An aggressor should only be taken to the ground for the purpose of gaining and/or maintaining control. Also, the aggressor should only be maintained in a prone position for the absolute minimum time necessary for your safety.

An aggressor may develop difficulty in breathing if kept in a prone position for a long period of time. In addition, it is dehumanizing to the aggressor.

Be careful not to add any more weight than is necessary on the aggressor and placing knees on the aggressor's spine or neck is **never** acceptable.

Now we will discuss how to control an aggressor from a prone position.

Prone Position Control Techniques

When the aggressor is in a prone position, the following techniques can be used for control. If resistance occurs during a control technique, you can go from one control technique to another until control is attained or you can disengage.

Straight Arm Control

When using this technique, you should be aware of compliance through verbal or non-verbal communications by the aggressor. Release pressure upon compliance, or injury to the shoulder, elbow, or wrist joint could occur.

Option 1: Place your hand on the aggressor's shoulder joint, lock your elbow, and use your body weight. Keep your arm locked and perpendicular to the aggressor's body.

The aggressor's wrist is bent 90 degrees with fingers pointing upward. Place your shin that is closest to the aggressor on the center of the aggressor's triceps and verbalize. A significant amount of your weight is on the ball of your foot.

To apply pressure:

■ Push down on the aggressor's triceps with your shin bone.

■ Push the back of the aggressor's hand (not the fingers) toward the elbow.

■ Have the aggressor extend the other arm away from the body with the palm up. This will reduce the aggressor's ability to resist.

■ The aggressor's head should be turned away from you. This will also reduce the aggressor's ability to resist.

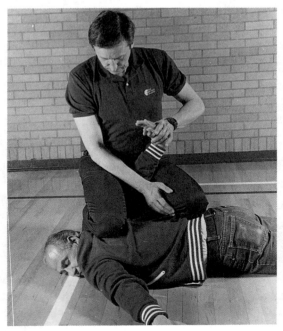

Option 2: Keep the aggressor's arm locked with the wrist bent and the fingers pointing directly towards the top of the aggressor's head.

▨ Your body weight should be on the balls of
your feet. Place one knee on the side of the
aggressor's back and the other knee on the
upper back or shoulder.

Do not apply any pressure on the aggressor's neck or spine. Your knees are used
strictly for stability and not for the application of pressure.

▨ Have the aggressor extend the other arm
away from the body with the palm up. This
will reduce the aggressor's ability to resist.

▨ The aggressor's head should be turned away
from you. This also reduces the aggressor's
ability to resist.

▨ To get compliance, verbalize and either:

 • Push the aggressor's fingers toward the
   head which applies pressure on the
   shoulder joint.

 • Push down on the back of the aggressor's
   hand (not the fingers) which applies
   pressure on the wrist joint.

 • Push against the aggressor's elbow with
   your forearm. This applies pressure on
   the elbow joint.

▨ Release pressure upon compliance.

These techniques have been proven to be extremely effective if you are smaller or weaker than
the aggressor.

Bent Arm Control

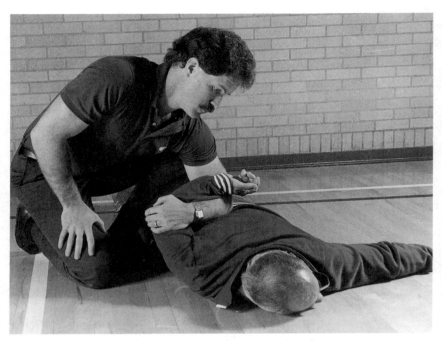

Place your hand on the aggressor's elbow with your thumb next to the index finger and place your elbow under the aggressor's wrist.

  Keep the aggressor's elbow and your elbow bent at least 90 degrees. Have the aggressor extend the other arm, palm up, away from the body. The aggressor's head should be turned away from you.

  Pressure is applied by pushing your bent elbow towards the aggressor's neck and pulling the aggressor's arm straight up from the back.

  Apply pressure to the back of the aggressor's hand by directing it toward the elbow, or pull up on the aggressor's elbow and wrist. **Caution:** Too much pressure will dislocate the aggressor's shoulder.

Bent Wrist Control

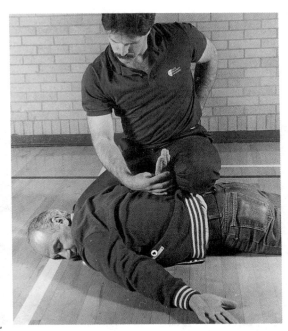

Bend the aggressor's elbow and wrist 90 degrees. Make sure the aggressor's elbow is held firmly against a solid object or between your knees.

Have the aggressor extend the other arm away from the body with the palm up and the aggressor's head should be turned away from you.

Apply pressure to the back of the aggressor's hand with your middle finger just above the aggressor's knuckles.

Pressure should be applied by pulling the aggressor's hand towards the aggressor's elbow or by pulling up on the aggressor's elbow and wrist. Release pressure upon compliance.

Depending on your authorization, after gaining compliance with one of the above techniques, another form of restraint, such as medication, handcuffs, or other restraints should be used.

22

Separating Two Aggressors

First attempt to neutralize a situation with dialogue and verbal direction. When confronting two or more aggressors, it is strongly recommended that assistance or backup be requested prior to making contact.

Approach the aggressor who is most aggressive from 45 degrees behind (the 2 1/2 position on Chart 1 in the Chart section).

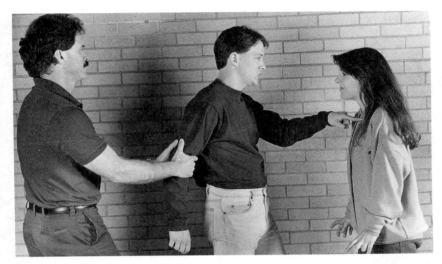

**Apply a blanket hold on the aggressor while verbalizing.
To take the aggressor off balance, pull downward on the
aggressor's arm at a 45 degree angle.**

**If resistance occurs and depending upon the level of
resistance, use the escort position.**

Separate the aggressors toward the 2 1/2 position (see Chart 1 in the Chart section) while keeping both aggressors within your vision.

If further aggression occurs, you should divert, escape, decentralize, and/or direct the aggressor to a prone position. Continuous verbalization is important.

Intermediate Intervention for the Physically Aggressive

Again, in any situation requiring a use of force, you must assess the level of the threat and determine the appropriate level of your response. Remember that deadly force is defined as any force you use that is likely to cause serious physical injury or death.

Approach the aggressor who is most aggressive from directly behind (position 3 on Chart 1 in the Chart section).

Place one of your hands on the crown of the aggressor's head and cup the aggressor's mouth with your other hand to prevent the aggressor from biting, or cup the aggressor's eyes with your other hand.

Apply pressure with your index finger to the aggressor's upper lip. Pressure is applied in the direction of your other hand that is on the aggressor's head.

Keep in mind that deadly force may never be used in defense of property. You can only respond with deadly force when you have determined that the threat level is likely to result in serious physical injury or death. Then, any force is acceptable that will deter the attack if it does not unreasonably endanger other individuals who may be present.

Pull the aggressor's head backward into your shoulder from directly behind (position 3 on Chart 1 in the Chart section). Keep the aggressor's balance broken to the rear and control the aggressor's head with your shoulder.

Keep your hips perpendicular or at a 90 degree angle to the aggressor. This will prevent you from losing your balance from the weight of the aggressor. It also makes it difficult for the aggressor to turn toward you.

Shuffle the aggressor backward while verbalizing. If further aggression occurs, you should divert, escape, decentralize, and/or direct the aggressor to a prone position.

Release pressure upon compliance and continuous verbalization is important.

Maximum Intervention for the Physically Violent

Approach the aggressor who is most aggressive from directly behind (position 3 on Chart 1 in the Chart section) and continuously verbalize.

Option 1: Strike the aggressor's tibial nerve center, which is 2 inches below the top part of the calf muscle (see Chart 3 in the Chart section), with the edge of your foot.

Option 2: Strike the common peroneal nerve center with your knee (see Chart 3 in the Chart section).

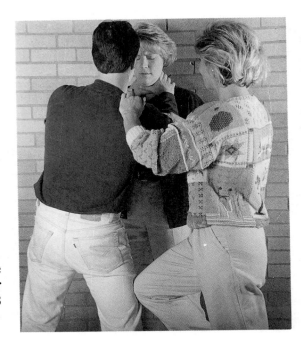

Option 3: Approach the aggressor who is most aggressive from the side. Strike the aggressor's lateral femoral nerve center with your knee (see Chart 3 in the Chart section).

Separate aggressors so that they are out of the sight of one another. If they are in an open area, separate them with a minimum distance of 22 feet between them.

Biography

Roland Ouellette, the author, is president and founder of R.E.B. Security Training, nationally known as a leading training company in law enforcement and security. Since 1983, he has provided training and consulting services to numerous law enforcement and correction agencies, corporations, hospitals, universities, colleges and the military.

Roland Ouellette

Roland is retired from the Connecticut State Police as a lieutenant and has served in the Army Security Agency. He was also a correctional officer for the Connecticut Department of Corrections and has conducted security and law enforcement courses at a Connecticut college.

Roland is well known for the development of the MOAB and OCAT® (Oleoresin Capsicum Aerosol Training) programs. For more information on this training, contact R.E.B. Security Training, Inc., P.O. Box 697, Avon, CT 06001, or call (203) 677-5936.

Footnotes

[1]"Days of Rage," (Special report on the Los Angeles Riots after the Rodney King Verdict), *U.S. News & World Report*, May 11, 1992, 20.

[2]Allan Pease, *Body Language* (North Sydney, Australia: Camel Publishing Company, 1981), 89.

[3]Samuel B. Griffith, *Sun Tzu, The Art Of War* (Oxford University Press, 1963), 89.

[4]Allan Pease, *Talk Language* (North Sydney, Australia: Camel Publishing Company, 1988), 49.

[5]James Turner, Ph.D., "Violence in the Emergency Department Video Seminar," *Emergency Nurses Association* (Pittsburgh, PA: Executive Communications, Inc., via satellite, October 15, 1991).

[6]"Whiteley vs. Warden," 401 U.S. 560, *Monadnock Lifetime Products PR-24® Instructor Notebook* (Fitzwilliam, NH: Monadnock Lifetime Products, Inc., January 1987), 189.

[7]"The Mental Edge," *U.S. News & World Report*, August 3, 1992, 54.

Chart 1

SPACE
(Proxemics)

POSITIONS OF
APPROACH

3

2 1/2   2 1/2

2   2

1   1

± 6' Social Zone

± 18' Public Zone

Grey Area = Reactionary Gap

= Danger — Stay Out

1 = Positions of Approach
2
2 1/2
3

Chart 2

CONFRONTATIONAL FORCE CONTINUUM

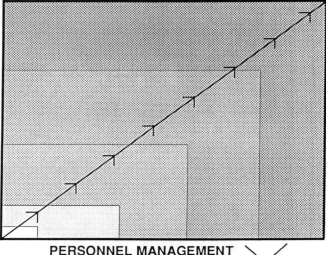

AGGRESSOR'S ACTION

<u>Losing Control Physically</u>
Static or Dynamic Assault With a Weapon

<u>Losing Control Physically</u>
Static or Dynamic Assault Without a Weapon

<u>Losing Control Verbally</u>
Verbal and Non-Verbal Threats

<u>Anxiety</u>

<u>Non-Aggressive</u>

Escalation of Force Based on Personnel/ Aggressor Factors

PERSONNEL MANAGEMENT

<u>Dialog</u>	<u>Persuade</u>	<u>Physical Defense/ Defensive Tools</u>

Non-Verbal
• Space
  4' to 6'
• Eye Contact
  Supportive
• Body Gestures
  Supportive
• Stance
  Supportive/
  Defensive
	Non-Verbal
	• Space
	  Greater than 6'
	• Eye Contact
	  Supportive/
	  Assertive
	• Body Gestures
	  Assertive
	• Stance
	  Ready
		Non-Verbal
		• Space
		  Greater than 6'
		• Eye Contact
		  Assertive
		• Body Gestures
		  Aggressive
		• Stance
		  Defensive

Verbal
• Verbal Skills
  Supportive
	Verbal
	• Active Listening
	• Verbal Skills
	  Direction/Set
	  Limits
		Verbal
		• Commands
		• Diversions

	Physical • Separate • Escort • Hands on Defense Tool	Physical • Escape • Divert • Defend • Use Defense Tool • De-Centralize • Direct to Prone • Control

Chart 3

Leg Nerve Centers

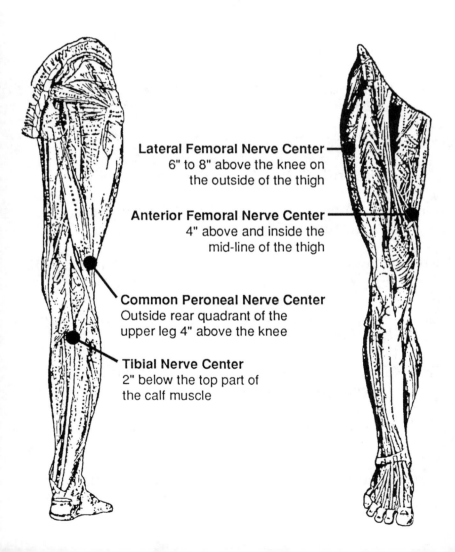

Lateral Femoral Nerve Center —
6" to 8" above the knee on
the outside of the thigh

Anterior Femoral Nerve Center —
4" above and inside the
mid-line of the thigh

Common Peroneal Nerve Center
Outside rear quadrant of the
upper leg 4" above the knee

Tibial Nerve Center
2" below the top part of
the calf muscle

Bibliography

Brown, Jr., Tom. *Tom Brown's Field Guide to Nature Observation and Tracking.* New York: Berkley Books, 1983.

Clede, Bill. *Police Nonlethal Force Manual.* Harrisburg, PA: Stackpole Books, 1987.

Cohen, Arthur. *Lethal Floor Fighting.* Hamilton, Ontario: Masters Publication, 1983.

Cunningham, William C. and Todd H. Taylor. *Private Security and Police in America.* Portland, OR: Chancellor Press, 1985.

Dunston, Mark S. *Street Signs.* Powers Lake, WI: Performance Dimensions Publishing, 1992.

Elgin, Suzette Haden. *The Gentle Art of Verbal and Self Defense.* Dorset Press, 1980.

Gawain, Shakti. *Creative Visualization.* San Rafael, CA: New World Library.

Griffith, Samuel. *Sun Tzu, The Art of War.* Oxford University Press, 1963.

Hibbard, Jack and Bryan A. Fried. *Weaponless Defense.* Springfield, IL: Charles C. Thomas.

Lorenz, Konrad. *On Aggression.* San Diego, New York, London: Harcourt Brace Jovanovich, 1966.

Morris, Desmond. *The Naked Ape.* New York:
   Dell Publishing, 1984.

Nierenberg, Gerald I. and Henry H. Clero. *How to
   Read a Person Like a Book.* New York:
   Pocket Books, 1971.

Nishiyama, Hidetaka and Richard C. Brown. *Karate.*
   London: Prentice Hall International, Inc.,
   1966.

Nowicki, Edward J. and Dennis A. Ramsey. *Street
   Weapons.* Powers Lake, WI: Performance
   Dimensions Publishing, 1991.

Oyawa, Masutatsn. *What is Karate.* Yokohama,
   Japan: Tokyo News Company, 1959.

Oyawa, Masutatsn. *This is Karate.* New York:
   Japan Publications Trading Company, 1965.

Remsberg, Charles. *The Tactical Edge.* Short
   Hills, NJ: Calibre Press, Inc., 1986.

Turner, Ph.D., James T. *Violence in the Medical
   Care Setting.* Rockville, MD: Aspen Systems
   Corporation, 1984.

Turner, Ph.D., James T. *Handbook of Hospital
   Security & Safety.* Rockville, MD: Aspen
   Publication, 1988.

Index

A

C

D

E

F

H

I

lungs   40

M

N

O

P

Q

R

U

W

Y

Other Books and Videos Available from Performance Dimensions Publishing

Con Games and Con Artists (Video): This program shows how some of the most popular confidence games are used on unsuspecting and trusting victims. Racine County, Wisconsin, Sheriff Eric Johnson, provides valuable insight into the methods and motivation of con artists.
ISBN: 1-879411-21-0. 27 minutes. $29.95.

Courtroom Skills and Tactics (Video): This video is meant to improve an officer's skills and abilities on the witness stand. Mark Baganz and John Livingston, two nationally known and well respected practicing attorneys, are featured. Meant for new and experienced officers alike, viewers are taken through a number of courtroom re-enactments that actually take place in a courtroom with an officer giving testimony. You have survived the streets, now learn how to survive the courts.
ISBN: 1-879411-16-4. 31 minutes. $29.95.

Crisis Intervention (Video): This program provides information on how to recognize and effectively intervene in a crisis situation. This program features Paul Roemer, a skilled and experienced hostage negotiator formerly with the Federal Bureau of Investigation. Viewers are also shown methods to de-escalate and resolve conflict that, if left unresolved, can lead to a crisis.
ISBN: 1-879411-20-2. 28 minutes. $29.95.

Interpersonal Communications Skills (Video): This video features one of law enforcement's most respected names, Ed Nowicki. This informative

program shows how to use and recognize voice inflection, body language, and proper distance to enhance the interpersonal communications' process. Learn why some of the most effective law enforcement officers are also great communicators.
ISBN: 1-879411-19-9. 29 minutes. $29.95.

Law Enforcement Ethics (Video): This video emphasizes the value of ethics for today's law enforcement professional. Containing live footage and interviews, the program offers much needed "food for thought." Neal Trautman, Director of the National Institute of Law Enforcement Ethics, is featured.
ISBN: 1-879411-17-2. 28 minutes. $29.95.

Street Signs (Book): Written by Mark S. Dunston, this is the most comprehensive identification manual ever written on symbols of crime and violence used by street gangs, hate groups, motorcycle gangs, prison gangs, and others as a secret method of communications. These street signs may be present in the form of tattoos, graffiti spray painted on walls, patches worn on clothing, or in many other ways. Street signs communicate a great deal about an entire group, or an individual group member. The *Street Signs* manual can be used alone, but it is best used in conjunction with *Street Signs: The Video* as a complete training and information package.
ISBN: 1-879411-13-X. 232+ pages. $14.95.

Street Signs (Video): This video visually dramatizes how many of the street signs shown in the book may put the uninformed at risk. Realistic and graphic portrayals will enlighten and amaze viewers. Although it can be used alone, this video is best used as part of a complete training and information package along with the book, *Street Signs*.
ISBN: 1-879411-12-1. 30 minutes. $29.95.

Street Weapons (Book): An identification manual for improvised, unconventional, unusual, homemade, disguised, and exotic personal weapons. *Street Weapons* is widely recognized as the most authoritative book ever written on these highly unusual weapons. This comprehensive manual contains hundreds of photos and drawings along with descriptions that clearly explain how these weapons can be used and carried covertly. Written by Ed Nowicki and Dennis A. Ramsey, two of the leading experts on these types of weapons. You will discover how a normal looking ring can turn into a deadly flesh tearing instrument, or how the stems to a pair of glasses can deliver deadly wounds. A companion to *Street Weapons: The Video*. Must reading for every law enforcement officer.
NOTE: This book will only be sold to law enforcement, security, corrections, or military personnel — proper identification required when ordering.
ISBN: 1-879411-11-3. 240+ pages. $19.95.

Street Weapons (Video): A companion to the book, *Street Weapons*. This fast paced video dramatizes the deadly potential of some of the weapons that are included in the book. Viewing this video should be mandatory for every law enforcement officer. Although this video can be used alone, it is most effective when used in cooperation with the book for a complete training and information package.
NOTE: This video will only be sold to law enforcement, security, corrections, or military personnel — proper identification required when ordering.
ISBN: 1-879411-12-1. 22 minutes. $29.95.

Supervisory Survival (Book): Written by over 20 different authors, this book provides a unique perspective on how to survive the rigors of supervision. The list of authors contains some of the most well known and respected names in law

enforcement. This books goes far beyond theory, it provides real and practical insights by experienced professionals. You've never seen a supervisory book like this. It is meant to be read by new, experienced, and aspiring supervisors.
ISBN: 1-879411-23-7. $17.95.

Total Survival (Book): One of the most unique books ever written about the important topic of officer survival. It is not meant to compete with, or to replace, any other books dealing with officer survival. It is meant to be a part of each law enforcement officer's survival library. The pages of *Total Survival* reads like a "Who's Who" in law enforcement training and writing. Over 45 authors contributed to this comprehensive survival source.
ISBN: 1-879411-18-0. 524+ pages. $24.95.

True Blue (Book): This critically acclaimed book contains "true stories about real cops." Written by one of the most respected law enforcement writers, Ed Nowicki, a twenty-four year law enforcement veteran who survived six shootings. *True Blue* contains an assortment of some of the most fascinating and compelling stories about the realities of being a law enforcement officer. This revealing book never lets up and will take you on a trip through the full range of human emotions. *True Blue* will have you uncontrollably laughing while reading one story and shedding tears while reading another. A provocative and sometimes shocking look into the extraordinary world of law enforcement. There's nothing quite like it!
ISBN: 1-879411-15-6. 255+ pages. $14.95.

Why Not Save Time and Order Now with Your MasterCard or Visa? Call TOLL FREE 1-800-877-7413.

Order Form

Telephone Orders: Call 1-800-877-7413. Have your MasterCard or Visa ready.

Postal Orders: Perormance Dimensions Publishing P.O. Box 502, Powers Lake, WI 53159-0502 U.S.A., (414) 279-3850.

FAX Orders: Fax your purchase orders to (414) 279-5758.

Qty.	Title	Price Each	Total
	Con Games and Con Artists (Video)	29.95	
	Courtroom Skills and Tactics (Video)	29.95	
	Crisis Intervention (Video)	29.95	
	Interpersonal Communications Skills (Video)	29.95	
	Law Enforcement Ethics (Video)	29.95	
	Management of Aggressive Behavior (Book)	14.95	
	Street Signs (Book)	14.95	
	Street Signs: The Video (Video)	29.95	
	Street Weapons (Book)	19.95	
	Street Weapons: The Video (Video)	29.95	
	True Blue (Book)	14.95	
	Supervisory Survival (Book)	17.95	
	Total Survival (Book)	24.95	

Shipping & Handling (a flat charge for any quantity)　　3.00

Total Enclosed　　　　　　　　　$

☐ Please send FREE information about other books and videos when published.

☐ I would like to host a Seminar.

Method of Payment:
☐ Check　☐ Money Order　☐ MasterCard　☐ VISA

If credit card: Card Number _____
Name on Credit Card _____
Signature _____Expires _____

Send to my :　☐ Work　☐ Home

Name _____Title _____
Agency/Company _____
Address _____
City _____State _____Zip _____
Agency/Company Phone ( )_____
Home Phone ( ) _____

WHY WAIT? Call your order in to us RIGHT NOW! Call Toll Free at 1-800-877-7413